D. J. Smith

Discovering Horse-drawn Vehicles

SHIRE PUBLICATIONS LTD

Published in 1994 by Shire Publications Ltd, Cromwell House, Church Street, Princes Risborough, Buckinghamshire HP27 9AA, UK.
Much of the text of this book and some of the illustrations were first published by Shire Publications in D. J. Smith's 'Discovering Horse-drawn Carriages' (first edition 1974; reprinted 1976; second edition 1980; third edition 1985) and 'Discovering Horse-drawn Commercial Vehicles' (first edition 1977; second edition 1985). The text has been revised, updated and extended for the present work, which also incorporates information from Mr Smith's 'Discovering Horse-drawn Transport of the British Army' (1977) and 'Discovering Horse-drawn Caravans' (1981).
 ISBN 0 7478 0208 4.

British Library Cataloguing in Publication Data: Smith, D. J. Discovering Horse-drawn Vehicles. I. Title. 688.6. ISBN 0-7478-0208-4.

Set in 9 on 9.5 point Times and printed in Great Britain by CIT Printing Services, Press Buildings, Merlins Bridge, Haverfordwest, Dyfed SA61 1XF.

Cover: *A garden-seat omnibus at the Science Museum, Wroughton, Wiltshire.*

Road transport contractor's heavy vanners.

Contents

ACKNOWLEDGEMENTS

The line drawings are by the author. The cover photograph is by Cadbury Lamb. Other photographs are acknowledged as follows: by kind permission of the Edgar Bates Collection, page 110; Keith Bennett, page 136 (top); Birmingham Museum and Art Gallery (photograph by Keith Bennett), page 48; M. H. Brindley, page 143 (top); N. Brindley, by permission of Hereford and Worcester County Museum, pages 132, 133; T. Edgson, page 45; General Post Office, page 51; Great Western Railway photograph, pages 116, 118 (top); Gunnersbury Park Museum, page 37; the HDV Series, pages 62, 65 (bottom), 80; the HDV Series, Co-operative Wholesale Society photograph, pages 98 (bottom), 101, 105 (top and bottom); the HDV Series, photograph by B. B. Murdock, pages 92 (bottom), 97, 99, 100, 102, 104, 106, 107, 108 (top), 125; the HDV Series, Savage Bros photograph, page 130; Hull Museum of Transport, pages 42 (top), 56 (bottom), 66 (bottom), 78, 87; A. Hustwitt, pages 90, 95, 108 (bottom); Imperial War Museum, page 136 (bottom), 137, 138; Cadbury Lamb, page 83; Raymond Lea, pages 49, 69 (top), 70; Leicestershire Museums, Arts and Records Service, pages 98 (top), 118 (bottom); London Transport Executive, pages 59, 60; the Mossman Collection, Luton Borough Council, Leisure and Amenities Department, Museum Services Division, pages 35, 36, 46 (top), 56 (top); National Shire Horse Centre, page 143 (bottom); by kind permission of the RASC Museum, Aldershot, page 134; by kind permission of Rothmans Ltd of Pall Mall, page 113; the Science Museum, Crown copyright, pages 65 (top), 69 (bottom), 71, 81; Robert A. Smith, pages 53, 131; Studio Sark Photos, pages 84 (top); Wally Talbot, page 92 (top); by courtesy of the Tyrwhitt-Drake Museum of Carriages, Maidstone, pages 40, 73; Marylian Watney, page 3; Brian Wicks, pages 33, 39, 42 (bottom), 44, 58, 72, 74, 79, 128; the author, pages 30, 34, 84 (bottom), 114, 117, 127, 142, 145.

Introduction

Transport studies form an integral part of social history. Animal haulage, particularly the use of horses and horse-drawn vehicles, was the dominant mode of transport until recent times. Today horses have been replaced by engines, but horse transport still has relevance for the modern age, mostly as a leisure pursuit. Perhaps as a reaction against over-mechanisation, there has been a revival of interest in both driving and the collection and restoration of horse-drawn vehicles. This trend is matched by increased opportunities to enter rallies, shows and events of national importance. Numerous transport and specialised carriage museums offer a wide range of vehicles, both on static display and for demonstration purposes, while several magazines are published by and for enthusiasts.

Although large numbers of horse-drawn vehicles were destroyed after the Second World War, merely to salvage scrap iron, many survived in roadworthy condition, while new types are being made and imported, especially for showing or competitive (cross-country) driving.

Those seeking a new interest in this sphere but who are not grounded in the traditions of the equestrian world may need to recognise different types of vehicle and to know something about their development. The difference between coach and carriage, car and cart or cart and wagon are but a few matters among those explained in the following pages, with notes on materials used, harnessing and driving.

Danish farm wagon.

1
Vehicle types

The earliest wheeled vehicles were either *carts* or *wagons* – even the chariot was a light but strongly built cart. Carts were always two-wheeled, while wagons were four-wheeled, irrespective of purpose, size or capacity. The cart, frequently used in rougher terrain than the wagon, had the advantage of rearward tipping and was more suitable for smaller loads with a single horse, as it took up less space and was more economical. The cart relied on shafts for draught connection, while wagons used either shafts or poles, according to the size of teams and method of harnessing.

Coaches were derived from wagons, the rumbling stage or carrier's wagon having much in common with the traditional harvest wagon or wain. Ancestral memories frequently associate wagon and coach with all that is solid and firmly established, while carts may be dismissed as cheap and tawdry. Controversy exists concerning lighter vehicles on two wheels, termed carts by some and *cars* by others, especially relating to the 'jaunting car', 'governess car' and 'ralli' or 'rally car'. 'Car' is a common noun in its own right, derived from the Latin *carrus*, meaning a type of chariot. It is not a contraction of either cart or carriage, although from the mid nineteenth century a range of village or rustic carts, especially those with superior finish, were known in fashionable circles as 'cars'.

To complicate matters further, certain light passenger vehicles on four wheels were known as *road wagons* or *carts*, especially in America. These might have been used for training, exercising and showing harness horses and were frequently open or semi-open. The term 'wagon' might also be associated with a version of the American buggy, referring to a sturdy type driven by business or professional men, rather than for pleasure. A typical example would be the 'doctor's wagon' used from the 1880s to the 1920s by medical practitioners, which had sufficient space for small items of luggage and a medical bag.

The name 'coach' is derived from the town of Kocs in Hungary, where four-wheeled passenger vehicles having many characteristics of modern types were constructed, especially from the late middle ages. Hungarians were descended from Magyar tribesmen who had migrated westwards from the steppes of Eurasia. At first nomadic keepers of flocks and herds, they made widespread use of wheeled transport and developed an enviable skill in crafting appropriate vehicles. Examples of their work were introduced via the trade routes of central Europe through Austria and Germany to Holland, France and Britain, although coachbuilding in western Europe was not firmly established until the mid sixteenth century.

The present definition of a coach is a four-wheeled passenger vehicle

Cheshire cart.

the head or cover of which is a fixed part of the bodywork.

Carriage derives from the Latin *carruca*, meaning a light pleasure or passenger vehicle, recognised as a medium to lightweight conveyance of superior quality. Most carriages are four-wheeled with falling or half-hoods, although the 'curricle' and 'cabriolet' of the early nineteenth century are exceptions as they ran on two wheels. In one sense all vehicles that carry passengers or goods may be termed 'carriages', while 'carriage' is also a shortened form of 'undercarriage', 'forecarriage', 'rear carriage' or 'hind carriage', meaning underworks and running gear. What may be termed 'carriage parts' are components of underworks.

Buggies were first related to the one-horse gig or cabriolet, being hooded, two-wheeled vehicles of European origins, but slightly smaller and less formal. Some had a rearward or groom's seat typical of the curricle. The later 'American' buggy was a tray-bodied vehicle, equirotal (the front and rear wheels being the same size) or nearly so, usually with a falling hood but sometimes almost fully enclosed – as seen in the later Amish buggy.

A *coupé*, also known as a 'chariot' or 'half coach', was a smaller or cut-down version of what might normally have been a larger vehicle. While the coach seated four, the coupé had seats for two passengers only, facing the direction of travel.

Numerous goods and commercial vehicles were drawn by horses and used in street deliveries or for carrying raw materials, often – during later years – in conjunction with other transport, their loads transhipped at dockside, canal wharf or railway siding. The *dray* was perhaps the best-known of these, confined mainly to town transport. It was usually a flat loading platform without sides, although some had upright stanchions and connecting chains to contain their loads. The earliest type of dray was a low-slung two-wheeled vehicle, used mainly by brewers to convey barrels of ale and porter. During the early nineteenth century it acquired four wheels, its team either led on foot or driven from a high seat above the forecarriage. Conversely the *float* began as a four-wheeler but ended up as a two-wheeled low-loader, usually on cranked axles.

Smaller versions of the dray, many appearing during the second half of the nineteenth century, might be known as a 'lorry', 'lurry', 'trolley' or 'rulley'. Unlike drays, some of these had brakes and low plank sides.

Trucks were covered vehicles on two or four wheels. Their name derived from the Latin *trochus*, meaning hoop, as they had their canvas tops supported by semicircular hoops or tilts. *Vans* developed from trucks and were mainly, but not always, headed.

Other commercial and utility vehicles such as *fire engines*, *water carts* and *timber tugs* or *carriages* need no explanation.

Some vehicles had strictly local names; the tub cart of most areas was also known as a 'Digby' north of the Tyne and a 'jingle' in the west of England. In the Yorkshire Dales and other northern areas a market cart was often referred to as a 'shandry'.

Country carts or carriages were strongly made but less smartly finished than the more fashionable types: the bodywork was varnished rather than painted, the latter treatment being reserved for wheels and underparts. They were also known as 'rustic' carts.

The name *trap* relates to a small, often cheaply made vehicle, usually a form of tub cart, in horse or pony size. In Britain it was a two-wheeler, but in America it frequently possessed four wheels. This description was widely used during the nineteenth century, although mainly in rural districts, but it was eventually considered a slang or vulgar term lacking precision. However, a popular light harness horse of the period was also known as a 'trapper'.

2
The early history of horse transport

In prehistoric times considerable use was made of the sleigh or slide-car as a means of conveying burdens too cumbersome for either humans or pack animals. The slide would be made from rough branches bound together with thongs of rawhide, with a basketwork container at its rear end. A forward-inclined projection of the slide formed an apex or 'A' shape, resting on the back of a draught animal, or even on human shoulders.

The wheel is thought to have been invented in either China or India, although the exact date is unknown. Disc wheels or perhaps rollers made from rounded cross-sections of tree trunks were an obvious solution to the problem of improved mobility. Crude discs, eventually attached to trailing ends of the slide, retained the basic 'A' plan, shafts or wagon poles appearing at a much later stage. A slide with added wheels was recorded in Spanish cave paintings of the third millennium BC.

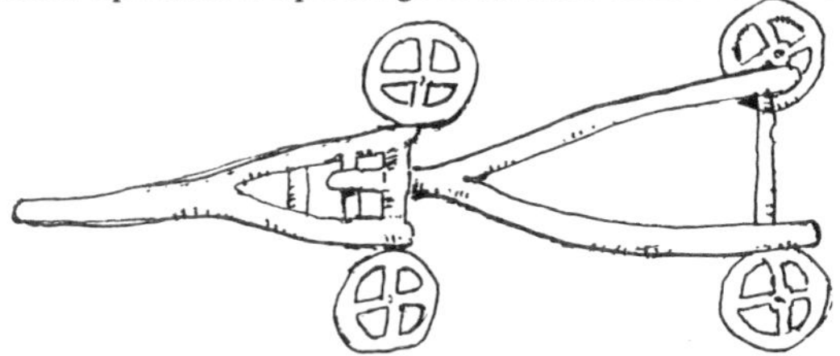

The double 'A' frame of an early wagon, from a Scandinavian cave drawing.

Early development of wheeled vehicles was greatly hampered by lack of good roads or serviceable tracks, especially in mountainous districts. There would have been greater scope for wheels on the rolling plains of central Asia, where nomadic tribesmen used headed or tented living carts, their covers made of crudely woven cloth or animal skins stretched over hoops.

Early vehicles were two-wheeled, with the exception of a Chinese cart or barrow where a single central wheel was surrounded on three or more sides by a ledge-like platform. Four wheels were a later development, at first associated with religious or ceremonial occasions and displays of wealth. Their box-like structure would be extended over 'H' or double 'A' frames between disc wheels. From their inception they were symbols of prosperity, associated with rich farmland and fertile plains, while two-wheeled carts were increasingly confined to backward, highland regions.

Wheeled vehicles, as we might recognise them today, are thought to

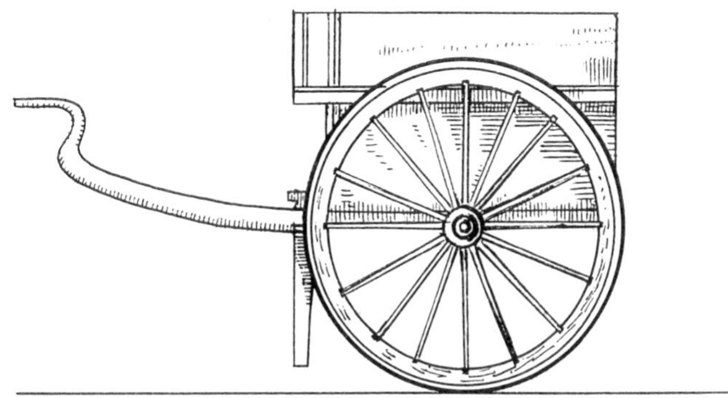

Chinese cart.

have appeared in the Far East between 2900 BC and 2000 BC. We learn of them from remains in burial places, especially toys and models, and also from contemporary wall paintings, carvings and bas-reliefs.

Ancient Egypt and the Middle East

In ancient Egypt most internal communications were made by river craft. Crude carts or trolley-like wagons, usually drawn by oxen in yoked pairs, were evident before the pyramids, but horse-drawn vehicles did not appear until the invasion of the Hyksos or Shepherd Kings about 1500 BC. These nomadic warriors came from the north-east to dominate Egypt, ruling both upper and lower kingdoms for over a century. Their military power depended on the use of swift war chariots, then unknown in the continent of Africa. Although eventually integrated with the Egyptians or driven out by them, the Hyksos taught their subjects to domesticate and train horses, which led to the development of superior Egyptian chariots and a wide range of greatly improved vehicles for

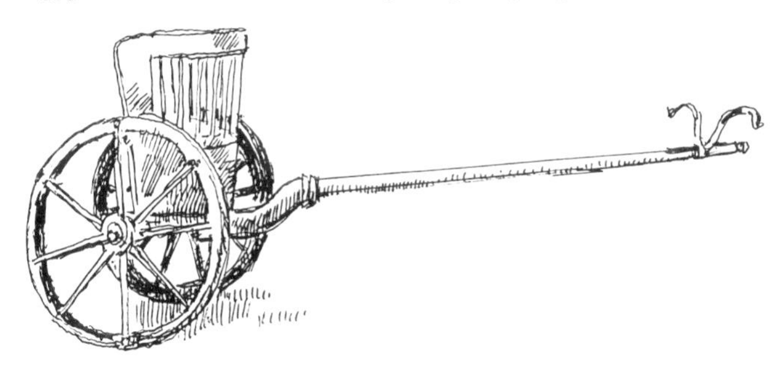

Egyptian chariot.

other purposes. The Egyptians were natural craftsmen and, by comparison with the cruder and heavier vehicles of the Assyrians, Babylonians and Sumerians, Egyptian chariots were elegant, lightweight but strong and free-running.

Early chariots were made of wood and leather, with tyres of hardened leather held in place by metal sprigs. All-metal band tyres were introduced by the Sumerians, but not reinvented until the mid eighteenth century. Harness developed from the neck yoke and pole gear originally used by a pair of oxen, but with additional neck and breast straps. From this evolved the neck and breast harness of modern Europe.

The Greeks and Romans

Evidence of both two- and four-wheeled vehicles, many of them chariots, has been found in Crete, dating from before 1500 BC. Their use eventually spread to the Greek islands and mainland, especially during the Mycenean period. Greek war chariots were larger than those of the Egyptians, although they had been greatly influenced by them. They were usually drawn by a pair of horses in pole gear, but later by three or more harnessed abreast. Wood and leather were still the main materials used, but wheels were frequently of bronze. There were races for specially constructed chariots at the Olympic Games, later extended to even larger teams in other sporting events. King Erectheus of Athens drove the first four-horse team, both in warfare and as a leisure pursuit. In all cases the yoke pole would be shaped or bent to suit the conformation of the horses in draught, while leather-bound arms extended from each side of the pole to bear on saddle pads, as the forerunner of 'curricle gear'. There would be a single pole to which a pair of the strongest horses of larger teams were attached. Other horses were harnessed to each other and the front of the chariot by trace ropes. Lydian chariots, introduced from Asia Minor, used a separate pole for each of three horses abreast, from which side shafts may have developed. Reins, especially those used

Roman chariot.

in chariot racing, frequently passed into a grooved ball on the pole, which improved the driver's control through greater purchase.

Open wagons and drays used by the Greeks, mainly for agricultural purposes, were frequently drawn by oxen, but later by mules. There were ceremonial cars and pleasure carriages, but these were not widely used as roads were badly made and there was little enthusiasm for them. Greeks able to ride on horseback considered the use of wheeled vehicles for passenger transport to be effeminate. Although some high-ranking ladies rode in a closed carriage or *apene*, men of all ages and conditions would scorn to enter anything on wheels, apart from chariots. Chariot racing was condoned not only for sporting purposes, but as a form of military training and character building, especially for younger men.

The Etruscans of northern Italy also made considerable use of chariots, copying their designs from Greek and earlier Egyptian types, although frequently including bronze wheels. Many of their chariots were high at the front and ran on large, nine-spoked wheels; others – especially those used for racing – had smaller wheels and were considered safer for cornering at speed.

The chariots of the Romans, used both for military purposes and for swift travel, were mainly responsible for their interest in road and bridge building, which brought about the development of civil engineering. This led to the expansion of an empire in three continents and an ensuing era of peaceful prosperity. The classical Roman chariot, a refinement of Etruscan models, was followed by a wide range of two- and four-wheeled vehicles for town and country. These included the *essedum* or fashionable carriage and the *carruca dormitoria* – a sleeping carriage or long-distance stage-coach, using slung hammocks for overnight travel. The Romans had no qualms about the use of wheeled passenger vehicles, finding them necessary for business, administrative and social enterprises. The simple dray-like *plaustrum*, one of the earliest Roman vehicles of the republic, was soon greatly refined and fitted out with upholstered cross-benches, on which governors, magistrates and other high-ranking officials toured the provinces. Such an important carriage would be known as a *sella curulis*, often headed, with a canopy roof. Lesser officials and citizens of lower rank travelled in a lighter, often two-wheeled, *carpentium*. A large baggage wagon with either plank or wickerwork sides, frequently used for military stores, was known as the *arccera*; many are depicted on the victory column of Trajan.

Fashionable young men drove about in a gig-like *cisium*, drawn by a single horse. Later versions were fitted with luggage racks and used as public carriages or cabs.

Most of the larger vehicles had sufficient clearance of the forewheels for limited lock, while some later types are known to have had hammock-type or slung suspension. Most vehicles, however, were unsprung or dead-axle, without brakes.

In the Celtic lands of western Europe, various types of chariot and carriage had already been developed before the Roman conquest. Both Britain and Gaul had versions of the *carruca* and the *essedum*, drawn by swift native ponies and driven with skill and daring. A larger version of the Celtic war chariot, sometimes with scythe blades attached to the wheel-hubs, was known as the *corvina*. Most British chariots, especially earlier types, were driven from a crouching position on the draught pole, which allowed the warrior-passenger greater scope for use of bow and spear.

The medieval period

Following the break-up of the Roman Empire there was a long period of stagnation, extending through what were known as the Dark Ages, well into the middle ages or medieval period. The magnificent network of roads left by the Romans was neglected or abandoned, communities becoming isolated and travel discouraged. As in the time of the ancient Greeks, wheeled carriages were despised by most people. The sick, elderly and certain ladies of high rank were carried in litters, slung between two beasts of burden or on human shoulders, but fitter people preferred to ride on a horse, ass or mule, according to their means. By this time highways had been reduced to rutted tracks, roughly paved only in or near towns.

However, towards the end of the middle ages there was a revival of both culture and commerce and better communications became necessary. As the population revived and increased after the ravages of the Black Death, feudal austerity gave way to material aims, expressed through a need for better living conditions. During the twelfth century the hammock wagon of the Roman Empire was reintroduced on a limited scale. During the reign of Edward II a crude passenger vehicle or 'long wagon' was introduced, also known as a 'whirlicote'. This had a long wheelbase and large equirotal wheels, drawn by teams of three or four horses in single file, guided by mounted drivers. The wheels were so large that underlock was impossible and the direction could be changed

Whirlicote.

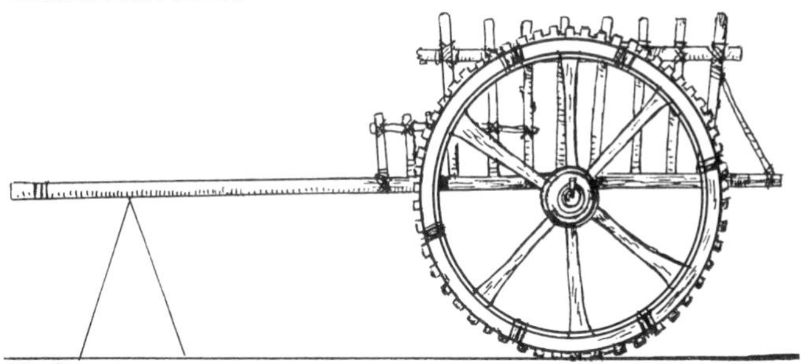

Medieval cart.

only by jerking the vehicle out of its ruts. Externally the whirlicote seemed magnificent, if ungainly, with its outer covering of richly embroidered tapestry supported by tilts. The interior, although dark and airless, might be furnished with hammock seats. Fractures and strains of the over-long bodywork were compensated for by the introduction of a strong underperch or reach pole, connecting fore and rear carriages. Problems of locking were eventually solved by the use of cranes or curved brackets, allowing clearance of forewheels in cut-under.

During this period vehicles for merchandise and agriculture were lumbering dead-axle types. Disc wheels, although gradually replaced by spokes, were shod with iron nails, which were eventually replaced by strips or strakes of iron. Bodywork and sides were frequently of wicker or basketwork rather than side planks or panels. The more advanced vehicles, both two- and four-wheeled, were used for military purposes,

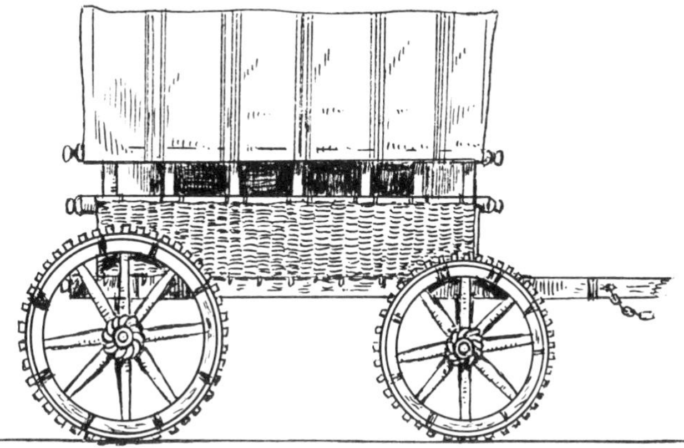

Medieval wagon with wicker sides.

culminating in the so-called 'Flanders wagon' and its derivatives. These were constructed with outwardly sloping sides, slung fairly low and drawn by a pair or team in pole gear. Many carts and wagons had their various parts held together with rope lashings.

In those days most inland goods traffic was handled either by river barges or, more usually, by packhorse trains. However, a few pair-horse wagons with tilted covers, sometimes guided by mounted drivers, were increasingly evident from the late fifteenth century. Such vehicles, with broad wheel treads, usually moved at a slow pace and were frequently led or driven on foot.

Until the early part of the sixteenth century it may be claimed that most vehicles were inferior to those of the Roman Empire, even the design of ploughs and agricultural implements.

The Renaissance

The period of the Renaissance, from the end of the fourteenth century, was remarkable for a gradual return of higher living standards, at first limited to the nobility and wealthier classes, but later affecting all ranks of society. This led to improved roads and better vehicles to travel over them. It was not, however, until the mid sixteenth century that travel in wheeled passenger vehicles became respectable for those fit enough to ride or walk as individuals.

The true coach, as opposed to the covered wagon and whirlicote, originated in eastern Europe. Its development and westward migration, partly influenced by parallel improvements in German wagon design – especially for military purposes – marked the beginning of a new era. There was universal acceptance of a strong underperch between fore and rear carriages with underlock and slung suspension. The use of primitive coaches, some little better than carrying boxes on wheeled platforms, spread throughout most parts of Europe but they were comparatively late in reaching France, Britain and Spain.

Early coaches in Britain were imported from Holland and Germany, at least until the late 1580s. The first coach designed and made on British soil was ordered for the Duke of Rutland in 1555 and constructed by the wagon builder or wainwright Walter Rippon. About 25 years later Henry Fitzallen, Earl of Arundel, imported a coach from Germany that was the envy of society and closely copied by those able to afford such luxuries. Queen Elizabeth I, not to be outdone by her courtiers, ordered several coaches from Dutch builders.

By the early seventeenth century there were not only private coaches for wealthy people but hackney coaches for public hire and a system of stage-coaches that plied between the larger towns. Yet in England it was over a century later before serious attempts were made to improve highways, which had been neglected in most areas since the Roman occupation. Land travel was hampered not only by threat of armed robbers but by quagmires and deep potholes in which vehicles might sink or break their axles. The near impossibility of long journeys in the depth of winter was partly responsible for the development of canals or inland waterways, for both goods and passenger traffic. The most effective, long-term solution was the development of the turnpike system of road repair and maintenance, while roads with improved surfaces, engineered by such men as Macadam, Metcalfe and Telford, were an incentive to improve the design of all vehicles.

Early coach developments

The first coaches were box-like and cumbersome, fairly low-slung but without proper doors or windows. Entrances and apertures were protected by leather curtains. What passed for a door would be at least partly blocked by sideways-on seating, occupied by a servant or fellow passenger of lower rank, their identity concealed by a protective velvet-lined iron mask. This mask was not only a precaution against attack but was also designed to ward off stones and mud churned up by the wheels. The first glass coach came from Italy to France in 1620, but there were few glazed windows, or lights, before the period of the English Civil War. The inclusion of fixed and later droplight windows, although first used in Italy, is attributed to a Frenchman named Bassompierre. The Infanta of Spain, consort of the Emperor Ferdinand, travelled in a leather-lined glass coach as early as 1631, but even Prince Rupert arrived at the battle of Marston Moor in an open-sided coach, of which there were still large numbers until the 1660s.

Coaches were greatly disliked by other road users and known as 'hellcarts' because they took up so much room, with their drivers

State coach of the Lord Mayor of London.

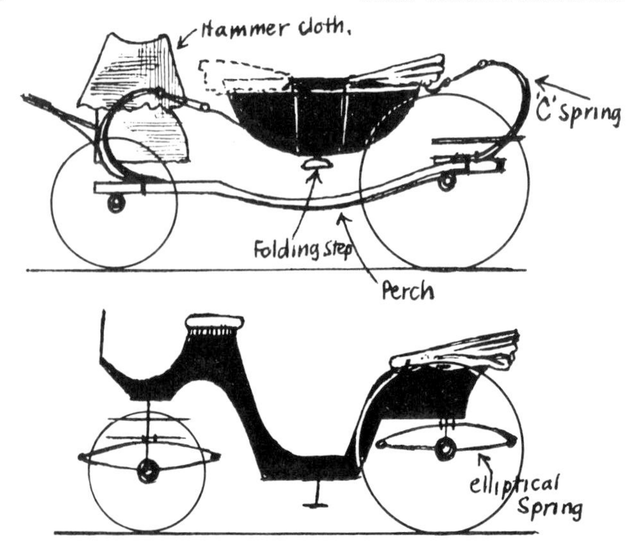

Above is an early carriage with underperch; below is a later type with elliptical springs, much lower, with no perch and a full lock.

demanding right of way for upper-class passengers. Also their heavy weight on narrow wheels made ruts deeper even than those made by baggage wagons. They would be drawn by large teams of horses and usually seated four or six inside, with two on the driving seat (box seat) and several footmen perched behind on a platform or dummy board. Towards the end of the seventeenth century smaller vehicles, for two passengers, drawn by a single horse or pair of horses, were known as 'half coaches', 'chariots' or 'Potsdams'. Potsdam was a city in the kingdom of Prussia, where such vehicles were first used in large numbers.

Iron springs were introduced to replace slings and braces in about 1670. They greatly reduced draught weight and unnecessary bulk, enabling vehicles to be higher, lighter and more elegant. The first springs were made of laminated iron, near upright or slightly curved, and known as whip springs; they were later replaced by elbow springs, which had more generous curves. Towards the end of the eighteenth century both were replaced by 'C' or 'cee' springs (also known as scroll springs) and later still by elliptical or semi-elliptical leaf springs. The eighteenth century was noted for reviving and perfecting inventions of earlier periods. 'Daleme' springing of the early eighteenth century was a combination of metal springs and strap suspension, named after the French clockmaker responsible for their introduction. A type of 'C' spring may be traced back to the seventeenth century but was little used until the 1780s. Attached between a jackbolt at the upper end of the laminated section, in horizontal form, and the actual bodywork would be adjustable loopstraps.

Wheels, tyres and axles

The correct type of wheel and its fitting was essential for all road vehicles. From the seventeenth century 'dished' wheels made a widespread appearance. 'Dishing' meant that wheels were cone-shaped and fixed to axle arms that inclined slightly downwards at the ends of each axletree. When revolving, the lower spokes were always vertical, thus taking the greatest stress. Dished wheels were claimed to be stronger and more reliable than straight or undished wheels, with spokes that were firmer and less likely to break loose. Eventually all wheels were at least slightly dished, especially those for heavy duty, many farm wagons having exaggerated dished wheels that contributed to their picturesque appearance.

Iron tyres were originally strakes or strips nailed to outer wheel rims in staggered (double) sections. Although metal ring tyres were known to the ancients, their use was neglected after the decline of the Roman Empire, but they were reinvented by an Englishman named Hunt in about 1767. Hunt's tyres were clamped round the wheel when red-hot, making a perfect fit as they shrank in the cooling-off process. Solid rubber tyres were introduced during the second half of the nineteenth century, fitting into a groove or channel of the wheel rim and later held in place by strong wires passing through the vulcanised rubber centres. Pneumatic tyres were invented slightly later but were not a commercial success until developed by a Scottish vet named Dunlop before 1889. Although used on some farm and many delivery vehicles during the 1930s, they were rejected by most coach and carriage builders as inelegant.

Axles formed a transverse rod or beam to which a wheel fitted at each end. They would be supported, as part of the undercarriage, by a solid

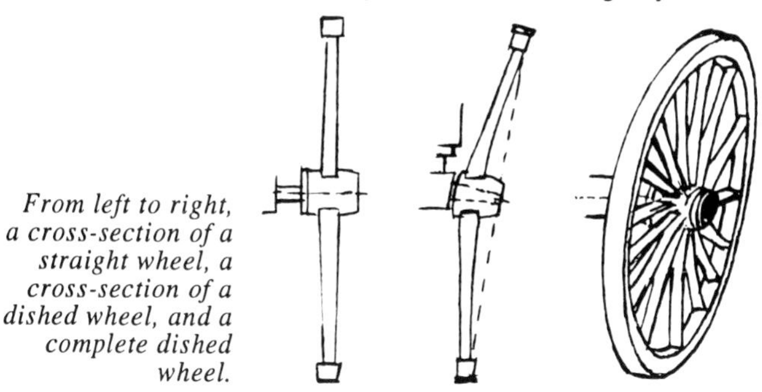

From left to right, a cross-section of a straight wheel, a cross-section of a dished wheel, and a complete dished wheel.

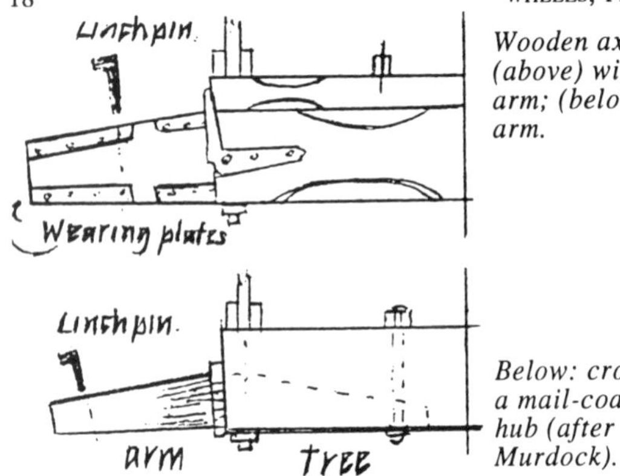

Wooden axletrees: (above) with wooden arm; (below) with iron arm.

Below: cross-section of a mail-coach axle and hub (after B. B. Murdock).

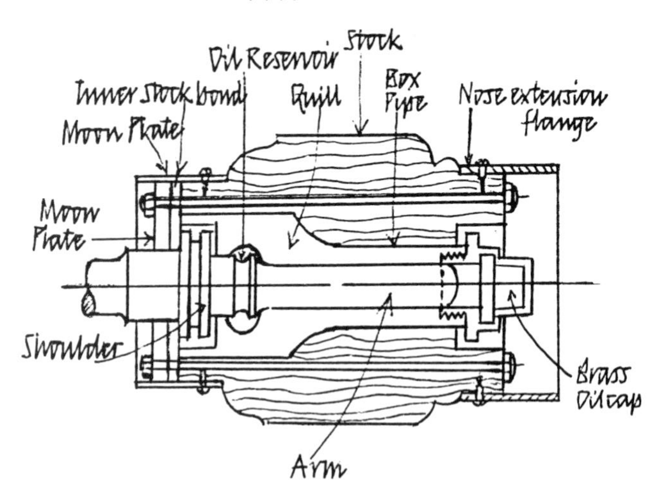

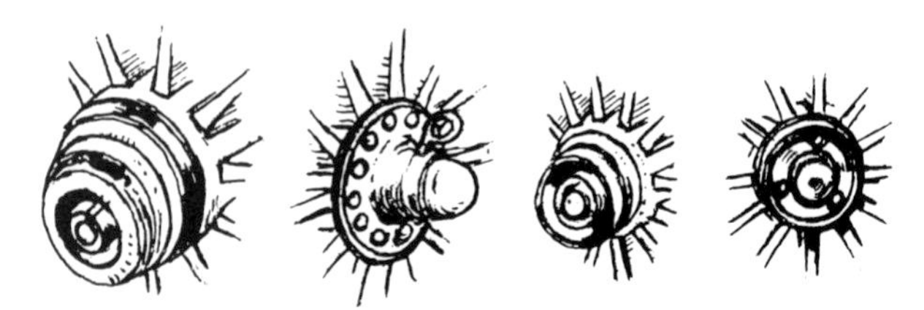

Hubs or naves (from left): wagon, artillery, collinge, mail-coach.

crosswise member or axletree. The common or drabble axle, used on many carts and commercial vehicles, was of the latter category, with each wheel fixed to its axle stub by means of a flat, wedge-shaped linchpin. Axles and hubs for 'superior' types of vehicle, usually coach or carriage, developed either as the mail-coach hub/axle or the collinge. Mail-coach axles were of patent design, the hubs attached by means of three exceptionally long screws – unlikely to snap at the same time, thus providing greater safety when travelling at speed. The collinge, sometimes misnamed the Collins, was also a patent, having cone-shaped hubs secured by external bands or collets and centre nuts. At the centre of each axle was a self-lubricating oil bath, hence its alternative name of 'oil axle'. Many later axles were a continuous iron or steel bar.

Draught gear

While smaller or single-horse vehicles had shafts (also known as thills), usually of the so-called 'lyre' type – wider at the rear end but narrower at the fore-end, conforming to the shape of the horse, most coaches, carriages and heavy wagons relied on pole gear. An exception would be farm wagons of the eastern counties with double shafts, in

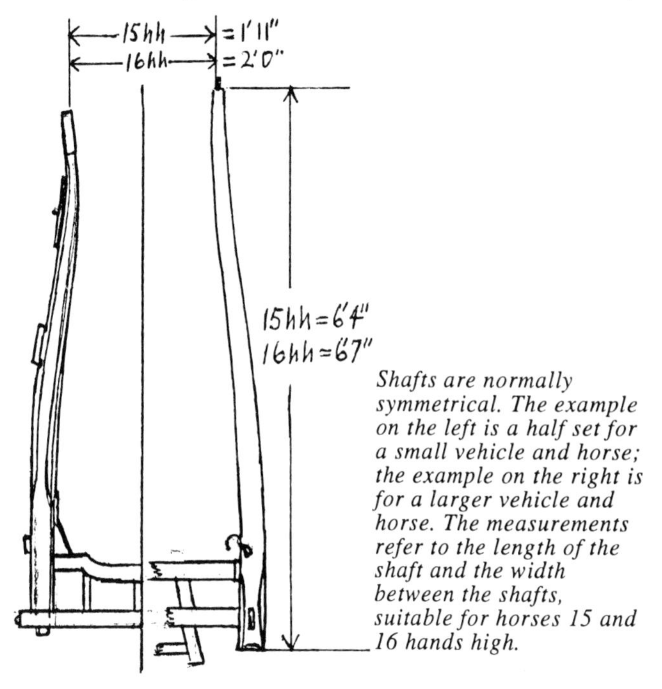

Shafts are normally symmetrical. The example on the left is a half set for a small vehicle and horse; the example on the right is for a larger vehicle and horse. The measurements refer to the length of the shaft and the width between the shafts, suitable for horses 15 and 16 hands high.

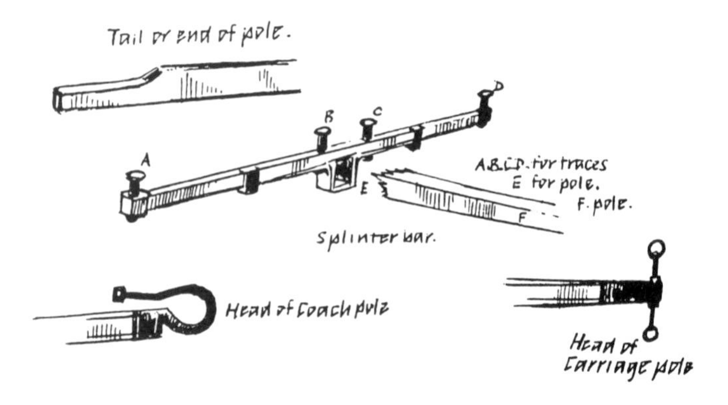

Draught gear.

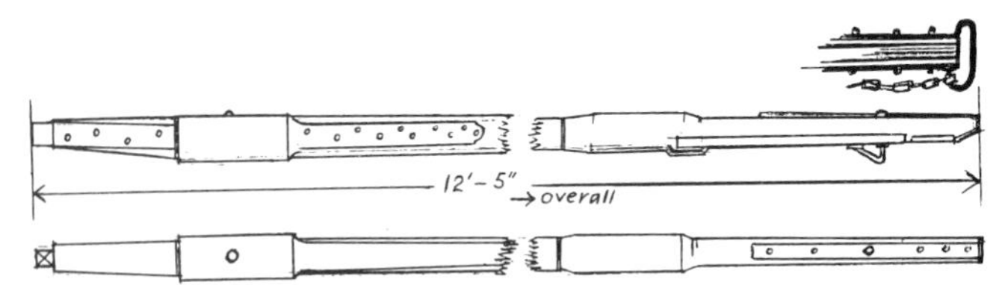

Wagon pole: (top right) alternative head of pole; (centre) elevation; (bottom) plan.

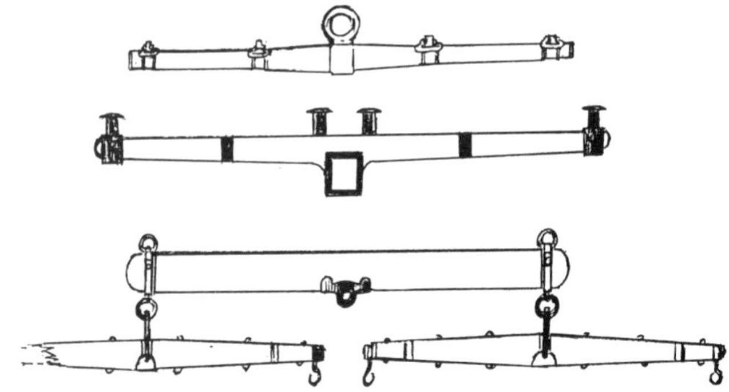

(Top) pole bar; (centre) splinterbar; (bottom) whippletree and swingletrees.

which two horses worked side by side, but not harnessed as a conventional pair. The use of double shafts, however, tended to make the beam of the vehicle too wide, a hazard when passing through gateways and barn doors. An alternative, widely popular for a heavy load, would be single shafts with an extra horse, the leader, hitched in tandem ahead of the horse next to the vehicle, the wheeler.

Wheel horses in pole gear were hitched one each side of the central draught pole. Traces, either leather straps or chains, led back to a crosswise or horizontal splinterbar at the front of the vehicle, often forming a projection of the forecarriage. The traces of coach harness looped round mushroom-shaped roller bolts or uprights on the splinterbar. Chain traces, especially on heavy wagons with pole gear, frequently connected not directly with the splinterbar but with a short horizontal bar or swingletree (one for each horse), hooked in turn to the fore-end of the vehicle. With teams of four or more, the leaders had swingletrees or draught bars attached to the head of the coach or carriage pole. A coach pole terminated in an elongated hook, at the end furthest from the vehicle, while a carriage pole, for lighter vehicles, had a pair of ring-loops. On a wagon pole there was, in most cases, a large, fully enclosed loop at the fore-end. When horses were driven as a tandem pair, or one behind the other, the traces of the leader connected directly with the harness of the wheeler, sometimes making use of horizontal draught bars.

Brakes and scotches

Although several types of brake were introduced from the early seventeenth century, very few proved to be of much value. They were considered worthless for two-wheeled vehicles, with rare exceptions, and until the nineteenth century hardly any attempt was made to use them on lighter vehicles. The most reliable form of check was the skidpan, shoe or slipper (known in country districts as a drugbat). This was an iron wedge or plate with a hollow centre, used to clamp the rear nearside wheel, to which it was attached on downward gradients. When not in use, the skidpan hung in chains under the vehicle. On some wagons, especially military types, a roller chained to hooks on the undercarriage could be adjusted, under the nearside rear wheel, to prevent it running backwards. A common check, frequently used when resting a team on an upward gradient, would be a rearward-pointing dogstick that dug into the ground to counter recoil. Many of the heavier shafted vehicles had a shaft prop or propstick hooked under each shaft, which could be lowered to support the cart when at rest. Chains were also hooked through rear wheels to lock them.

During the first half of the nineteenth century both pedal and hand brakes were introduced, followed by a manually operated screw-down brake. Brakes, especially the screw-down types, were usually applied

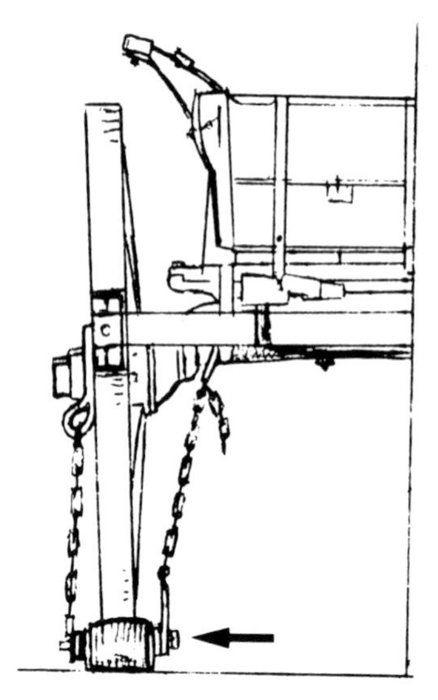

Roller scotch (arrowed) chained to prevent the wheel running back.

when horses stood for long periods and became impatient, particularly when not under the control of a driver or groom. The manufacture of hand and foot brakes was a highly skilled craft akin to axle making – it was the domain of specialist craftsmen who took great care to prevent rattle or vibration. From the second half of the nineteenth century it was recognised that vulcanised rubber was the best material for external blocks clamped on metal tyres, while a combination of wood and cast iron served better on solid rubber tyres. The long connecting bar of the hand lever brake was eventually replaced by a lighter more convenient Bowden wire, passing out of sight through the bodywork of the vehicle. During the 1930s disc brakes were used on certain delivery vans, especially those needed by the parcels express departments of main-line railway companies.

Later developments of suspension

After extensive use of 'C' springs the next stage of development was based on elliptical or semi-elliptical leaf springs; these were eventually to become the main form of suspension, allowing coaches in particular to be even lighter and less cumbersome. Large vehicles continued to retain their underperch, but small and medium-sized vehicles had the underbody reinforced with metal bars or plates, forming a connection between fore and rear carriages. This, in conjunction with a forward or semi-detached projection of the box seat, often above a rounded or turtle-backed boot, allowed space for improved underlock of the smaller front wheels.

The late eighteenth century

During the second half of the eighteenth century there was not only an improvement in roads but a greater variety of vehicles using them. This era saw the emergence of phaeton, barouche, landau, travelling chariot or postchaise and gig, most of which survived in some form or other into the first half of the twentieth century. By 1775 there were four hundred registered stage-coaches, while numerous hackney coaches (frequently discarded town coaches of the nobility) plied for hire in city streets. During the middle of the century a coach journey between London and Manchester took four and a half days, but in less than fifty years, owing to improved roads and vehicles, this time was reduced to eighteen hours.

Throughout the seventeenth and eighteenth centuries and well into the nineteenth century large and often elaborate coaches were constructed for royalty, the nobility and wealthy private owners. The Speaker's coach, still appearing in state ceremonial, dates from the late Stuart period, while in 1757 a coach was constructed for the Lord Mayor of London (the present coach is an exact replica of this). In 1761 the State Coach of England was ordered for the wedding of George III and it has been used at every coronation since 1820. Such vehicles had ornate carved and painted panelling, the box seat draped with a fringed and embroidered cover or hammercloth. These were known as 'state' coaches or 'dress' coaches because they were used on formal

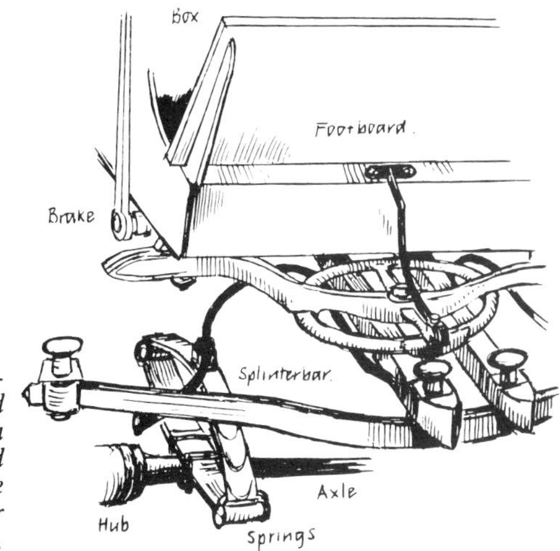

The fore-carriage and undergear of a four-wheeled vehicle suitable for two or four horses.

Early nineteenth-century state coach.

or 'full-dress' occasions, seating four people vis-á-vis as opposite pairs. Less formal coaches in daily use were known as 'town' coaches (unless adapted as 'travelling' coaches for long-distance driving). Coaches designed for European royal or imperial families during this period are works of art, among the treasures of our common heritage. Perhaps the most impressive were commissioned by the Austrian House of Hapsburg; they are still on show at the Imperial Carriage Museum, Vienna. The state and coronation coaches used by Napoleon I are also admirable of their kind, although by the early nineteenth century styles were becoming more utilitarian.

Barouche.

Light, swift carriages, many owner-driven, developed towards the end of the eighteenth century, followed by the introduction of 'curricles' and their unique style of harnessing. The curricle and its gear were, in some ways, a return to the Greek and Roman mode of chariot driving, which had lingered in continental Europe. It was a form of draught based on a centre pole which had T-shaped arms or extensions resting above the pad saddle of each horse, aiming to keep them in close, level action, although the main draught was through traces from neck collars to a pair of draught bars or swingletrees. This type of carriage was used for swift, light work; it was noted for its lack of noise or vibration and was much safer than contemporary and slightly earlier phaetons.

The nineteenth century

In the opening decade of the nineteenth century the use of two-wheeled as opposed to four-wheeled owner-driven vehicles increased, especially among fashionable younger people. While the curricle at

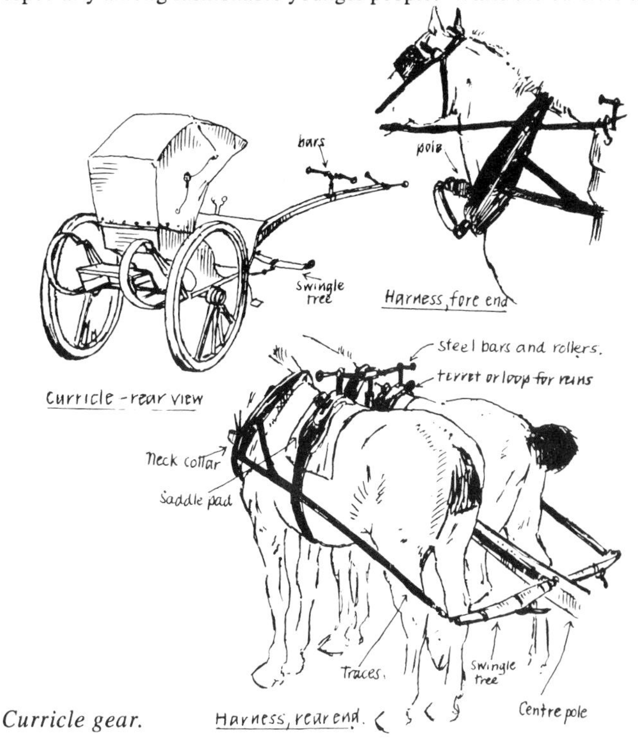

Curricle gear.

first seemed predominant, this was challenged by the cabriolet (which was even lighter and lower), drawn by a single horse. 'High-flyer' phaetons driven either to a pair or a four-in-hand team were gradually ousted, this partly reflecting a change in fashion influenced by the Prince Regent, later George IV. As the Prince grew older he became stouter and less agile, unable to cope with the difficulties of entering or driving a high-perched phaeton. The popular demand was still for speed and personal control, but with less risk and greater comfort.

As the century progressed, town and dress chariots, being more compact versions of the travelling chariot, began to replace coaches. These seated two passengers rather than four but were considered lighter and more comfortable than coaches.

Stage and mail coaches, both with roof seats and improved or 'Telegraph' suspension, were at the peak of their performance and viability during the first thirty years of the nineteenth century. This was also the great age of amateur driving, an enthusiasm kept alive even after the domination of the railways by such organisations as the Four-in-hand Club, the Bensington Club, the Four Horse Club and the still active Coaching Club.

Omnibuses, first invented and used in Paris, were brought to England by George Shillibeer, a former naval officer turned coachbuilder, in 1829. The hansom cab, designed as a patent two-wheeled vehicle, was the brainchild of Joseph Hansom, an architect. The four-wheeled cab or 'growler' (so named after the creak of its bodywork and the rumble of iron-shod wheels) appeared in London about 1840, adapted from a family coach known as the clarence.

Perhaps the most popular but the smallest of coachman-driven vehicles was the brougham, designed for and named after the Whig statesman Lord Brougham. This appeared in 1838-9, although a lighter more elegant version did not appear until several years later. The brougham was the last original type of coach or four-wheeled carriage, especially popular with those living in modest style. Other popular passenger vehicles of the middle to late nineteenth century, such as the victoria, wagonette and brake, were mainly derived from earlier vehicles of the same type.

From the mid century onwards a wide range of specialised vehicles served the increasing needs of trade, agriculture, industry and public utilities, all of which are considered in separate chapters.

3
Methods of driving

A passenger or pleasure vehicle with four wheels was usually driven from a raised or box seat above the forecarriage, although a few of this type, including the village phaeton and sociable, could be driven from the interior by an owner-driver. The box was originally a tool chest in which a repair kit might be kept, but later used for the storage of valuables. On the state or dress coach it was covered by an elaborate fringed hammercloth protected by a waterproof sheet in wet weather. At one time formal or more expensive vehicles were known as 'hammercloth coaches'.

Smaller types and the majority of two-wheeled vehicles had a combined driving and passenger seat for two, usually with a back rest, the driver sitting on the right-hand or off side. A few vehicles had a single or solo driving seat and were known as 'sulkies'; this type was considered anti-social. A rare vehicle known as the 'Punch carriage', because its upper-rear part resembled a Punch and Judy show, had a single box seat facing in one direction and a double or single passenger compartment, semi-open, facing in the opposite direction. The latter was said to have been favoured by those allergic to the odour of horses. With the later type of two-wheeled float (especially those intended for light delivery purposes but also able to carry passengers), the governess car and the tub cart, both driver and passengers entered through a rear door and sat on lengthwise or cross-seats, well back in the body of the vehicle. Floats, being fairly low, on cranked axles, were often driven from a standing position, affording a better view of the traffic ahead. In the governess car or tub cart the driver might sit turned on a lengthwise seat on either side of the vehicle, halfway down its length. Allowance was made for this by cut-away sections in the common seat (shared with a passenger on each side) into which the legs might fit. This made the car awkward to control, although only the smallest and most reliable ponies were expected to fit between its up-curved shafts. Rare exceptions to the rule could be found in versions of both float and governess car with front rather than rear entrances. With floats the rearward entrance would be necessary in loading milk churns and market produce from road level. Governess cars were essentially for young children and a back door was much safer for tiny feet than shaft steps near the hindquarters of the pony. Tub carts – as a cheaper, perhaps slightly larger and more popular version of the governess car – were driven by elderly, less agile people, especially in country districts.

Heavy commercial vehicles and wagons used for agriculture were frequently led on foot, but they could be driven by standing in the body of the vehicle, or by walking, with long reins, on the near side. Harvest wagons in east Yorkshire (the East Riding, now mainly Humberside) were drawn by two, three or four horses in a version of pole gear, a mounted wagoner astride one of the wheel horses. During the nineteenth century many gypsy living vans were driven on long reins from the roadside, although this was discouraged, if not forbidden, as unsafe and likely to cause traffic delays.

Lighter commercial vehicles, especially delivery vans, would be driven from a cross-bench or seat above the forecarriage, feet usually supported by an angled footboard or low toeboard. Some larger vehicles such as the furniture van and brewer's dray had an elevated or box seat supported on brackets.

In country districts a cart or wagon was sometimes driven from a sideways-seated position on a nearside shaft; this was considered dangerous in most circumstances, but foolhardy in town traffic!

Postilions

Some carriages and coaches on a good road, especially the travelling chariot and postchaise, were often controlled by mounted drivers or postilions, riding the nearside horse and driving its offside partner. Mounted drivers, less frequently in charge of heavy horses drawing baggage wagons, also controlled teams harnessed to the whirlicote or long wagon of the thirteenth century. In the latter case horses would be hitched in line or one behind the other rather than in pairs. With the whirlicote team alternate horses, numbering up to five, were ridden, the lead postilion being on the second horse, guiding it and the leader with whip and voice. This kind of wagon was awkward and lumbering, its rate of travel seldom more than an ambling trot, yet anything faster, with such large wheels and restricted lock, would have been highly dangerous.

On the continent postilions driving a pair or larger teams of swift horses attached to lighter carriages (at least from the early eighteenth century) were highly popular and known as *à la d'Aumont*, said to have been introduced by the Duc d'Aumont. Continental roads, at least until the mid eighteenth century, were constructed for military purposes and thus were much better for speeding than British highways. Driving from the box by coachmen was the slower but safer British method. Fast driving in Britain came during the closing decades of the eighteenth century as roads gradually improved, usually in owner-driven phaetons as a leisure pursuit. When a team of four or more was hitched to a phaeton (or larger vehicle), one of the lead horses would be ridden by a postilion.

The system of hiring postchaises from inns and road houses, as a more exclusive alternative to the stage-coach, was developed during the late eighteenth century. A pair of hired horses would be in the care of a postboy or mounted driver of any age from sixteen to sixty. Yet even at the height of its popularity 'posting' was considered more a European than a British mode of travel. Very few travelling or town coaches of the British upper classes were driven *à la d'Aumont*, the dignified but

Postchaise, c.1795.

frequently cross-grained family coachman remaining a key figure in domestic service for two and a half centuries.

The reason why traffic in Britain drives on the left is that most people are naturally right-handed and coachmen driving British teams or pairs sat on the right of the box, when this was shared with a groom or footman. The postilion or postboy rode on the near or left-hand horse, using the whip on its offside companion. It was a natural preference to keep a ridden horse nearer the crown of the road than the gutter, but when postilions were outnumbered by coachmen they had to obey the rules of the majority. The thirteen rebel colonies of North America changed to left-hand drive during the War of Independence, perhaps in deference to their French and continental allies.

Harnessing teams

The usual methods of harnessing driven horses were: singles (one horse in shafts); pairs (two horses in pole gear, but less frequently in double shafts); tandem (two horses, one behind the other); trandem or troika (three horses abreast, also known as the Manchester hitch or harness); pickaxe (one horse behind and two or more in front); unicorn (two horses behind and one in front); four in hand (one pair in front – the leaders – and one pair behind – the wheelers); and sixes (three pairs in line). There was no upper limit to the number that could be driven, apart from the constraints of roads and traffic. However, a team of more than four horses was rarely seen, except for ceremonial purposes, after the mid eighteenth century. For circus and carnival parades, especially in the United States, a forty-horse hitch has been recorded. It was also possible to use forty or more horses (or mules) to draw early examples of the combine harvester, before tractors and self-powered types were introduced.

On steep hills vehicles were frequently assisted by an extra horse in front. This was known as a 'cock' horse when used with coaches and buses and as a 'chain' horse (because it used chain traces or 'chains') on heavy wagons. Early buses on the streets of Paris were drawn by three horses abreast, as were the first London buses introduced by Shillibeer. The Russians frequently drove three horses abreast in a troika, although only the centre horse was in draught and a trot, the outer horses merely cantering for show with arched necks and heads inclined outwards.

Military horse ambulances, used for the recovery of sick and wounded horses, were normally drawn by a single horse in shafts. They had an extension bar on the nearside to which a ridden (extra) horse might be attached, hitched via a swingletree. Gypsy caravans had a similar extension bar on the offside, to which a young horse or 'sider' might be attached, partly to share draught but mainly for training purposes.

From the late eighteenth century daring young men drove high-seated gigs and cocking carts to a pair of horses in tandem ('tooling a tandem'). This was dangerous in traffic and where there were many road junctions; it was safe only in parks, on private roads or in the show ring. Although such daring was less popular in staid Victorian Britain, there were always a few prepared to drive in this manner and there was a revival of this technique for show purposes around 1900. Even today there may be the chance to see a gig or dogcart driven tandem in light-harness classes at a national horse show. Only two-wheeled vehicles are driven tandem. Some later cocking carts, after a brief revival towards the end of the nineteenth century, were driven to a pair of horses or three horses abreast in pole gear. Other vehicles harnessing a pair in pole gear would be the curricle and South African 'Cape cart', the latter using a form of harness based on belly bands or 'bugles'. In India the native ekka cart depended for draught connection on a triangular structure resting on the back of a horse or pony, rather than side shafts.

Driving unicorn.

4
Coachman-driven vehicles

From this stage onwards it is necessary to separate different types of vehicle for closer study, owing to a greatly increased diversity.

Coaches or carriages driven by professional coachmen were four-wheeled and usually much heavier than owner-driven carriages. Some of the lighter types would be drawn by a single horse but the majority were handled by a pair or four-in-hand. A useful distinction can be made between travelling carriages or coaches for long-distance work and town coaches used for shorter distances; the latter can be subdivided further into those suitable for formal occasions and less formal types in daily use.

The berline

The berline or berlin first appeared during the 1660s and its invention was attributed to several individuals, including a Frenchman named Roubo, but later to an Italian, Phillip de Chiese, employed as civil engineer by the Duke of Brandenburg. The first vehicle of this type had two underperches in parallel, high enough at the fore-end for full underlock. It is worth noting that with the single or central underperch on other vehicles the turning circle was strictly limited. This style of coach was first used in the city of Berlin, from which its name derives. Neglected for a number of years, it was restored to favour in both Germany and France during the mid eighteenth century. Sideways motion or lateral sway of the body was checked by adjustable leather straps attached to the undergear at each of the four corners. The berline was used for long-distance travel and more formal occasions, having a

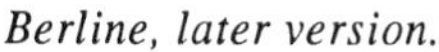

Berline, later version.

rearward platform (dummy board) for two or more footmen. The box seat was very high above ground level to allow for underlock. It was drawn by either two or four horses.

The halberline

A coupé or cut-down version of the berline, mainly popular during the 1780s, the halberline seated two passengers facing forward, similarly to the travelling chariot, postchaise or state chariot. The forewheels were much smaller than those of the berline, while the box seat was comparatively lower. It was mainly used for semi-formal town driving.

Vis-à-vis.

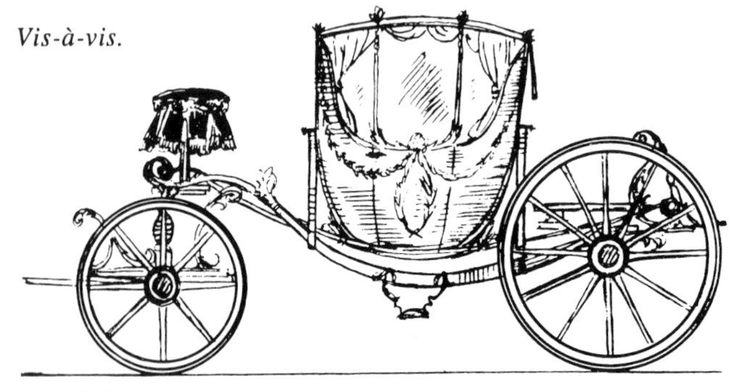

The vis-à-vis

A narrow version of the berline, the vis-à-vis was suitable for two people facing each other on opposite cross-seats. First popular about 1768, it was reintroduced into England, for a short period, about 1818, but few survived the reign of George IV (1820-30). The term vis-à-vis was also applied to any passenger vehicle in which the occupants sat facing each other.

The landau

In its original form the landau was imported from Germany during the late eighteenth century. It was a semi-open carriage with double half-hoods that could be closed against each other, for use in all weather conditions. On early vehicles the half-hoods were made of harness leather and fell back, when lowered, at an angle of 35 degrees. In wet weather, with hoods raised, the interior would be uncomfortably hot, made more oppressive by the smell of oil and blacking used to keep the leather flexible. Bodywork of early types was square and inelegant; floors dropped to a much lower level than the seating, which was untypical of the period and continental designs in general. More elegant later types, with curved or contoured bodies, were known as 'Sefton' or 'canoe' landaus. From the mid nineteenth century great improvements

Landau.

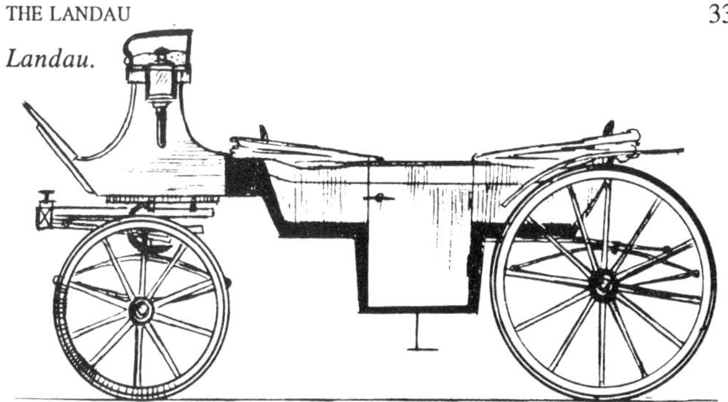

were made in hoods, which eventually folded flat. An improved square landau was known as the 'Shelburne'.

Landaus could be drawn by a single horse in shafts but were usually driven to a well-matched pair in pole gear. They held four passengers vis-à-vis, with room for a coachman and a groom on the box seat. A larger version, known as the state landau, several of which have been in royal service, have rumble seats for two footmen. These would be drawn by four horses *à la d'Aumont.*

Both Sefton and Shelburne types were at first hung on 'C' springs, but later on elliptical springs or a combination of both. Early or larger landaus frequently retained the underperch. A Sefton landau around 1900 could be purchased from £200 upwards, according to trim. Like many four-wheeled open or semi-open carriages, the body of the landau was reinforced on the underside with a steel plate.

Sefton or canoe landau.

Landaulet.

A coupé version, known as the 'landaulet', seated two people facing forward. This appeared during the 1800s and remained popular throughout the greater part of the nineteenth century. It was drawn by a single horse in shafts or a pair of large ponies in pole gear. The landaulet featured a rearward half-hood that might close against a front panel or windscreen and was raised or lowered in sections. During the late Victorian era this type of vehicle was identical with a country cab known as the 'station fly'.

A later, full-sized version, known as the side-light or five-glass landau, had a forward structure similar to the landaulet. It had glass panels that could be raised, in place of the fore-hood, headed by an extension of the rearward half-hood. This improved interior light and vision but was far more expensive than other types.

The barouche

The name 'barouche' is derived from the Latin *birotus,* meaning two-wheeled. In ancient times a barouche was a small pleasure cart or gig, but it developed into a larger, four-wheeled vehicle. Both French and German versions were available and some of the latter were introduced to Britain as 'German wagons'. These had full undergear and low quarters or side panels but only a rearward half-hood. Passengers normally faced in the direction of travel, as in a chariot, but some barouches had folding seats in the forepart, on which two people might sit vis-à-vis. A semi-formal carriage, driven in both town and country, its high box seat was placed above a rounded or turtle-backed boot. It was drawn by a pair or larger team, in the latter case *à la d'Aumont,* with its box removed. In wet weather raised panels or upper quarters (lights)

Barouche c.1830 in the Mossman Collection at Luton, Bedfordshire.

set on the forepart could be closed against the half-hood. Early versions hung on 'C' springs, but these were later combined with or replaced by elliptical leaf springs. Most had either a rearward dummy board or rumble seat for carriage servants. Nearly all versions retained the underperch.

The calèche

The calèche was a version of the barouche known as the *Kalesche* in Germany and the 'calash' in Britain. It was usually drawn by a pair of horses in pole gear. A slightly larger version with complex cross-springing was known as the 'eight-spring calèche'; it could be adapted as a travelling carriage and was popular in the Atlantic regions of the American colonies. There were both 'C' and elliptical springs and a box large enough for coachman and groom. Four passengers were normally seated vis-à-vis. The original version had a strong underperch.

In North America a two-wheeled gig or chaise was also known as a 'calèche'; it was particularly popular in the French Canadian provinces, with a version also appearing on Nantucket Island, New England.

The travelling chariot and postchaise

The travelling chariot was a less refined but slightly larger version of the town or state/dress chariot. It was originally a gentleman's carriage or closed chariot adapted for long-distance travel. The postchaise developed from this. It was frequently used for a grand tour of continen-

Postchaise.

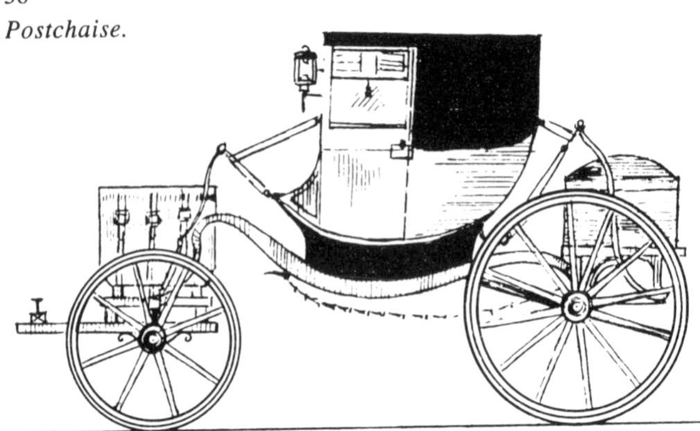

tal Europe, with door panels emblazoned with a family crest or monogram. A notable feature would be a horizontal sword case (for dress swords) at the rear of the passenger compartment. The travelling chariot, unlike the postchaise, frequently had a rumble seat for family servants. Either two or four horses would be used, guided by postilions, although a few may have had a high box seat. Horses were usually hired from inns and posting houses at various stages of a long journey. Mounted on 'C' springs, it had a strong underperch. It was mainly popular between the 1780s and 1830s.

Many postchaises were former travelling chariots, although extra

State chariot c.1790 in the Mossman Collection, Luton.

A posting chariot, probably built in Austria at the end of the eighteenth century, and used by Nathan Meyer Rothschild. Now in Gunnersbury Park Museum, London.

luggage space was made by replacing the rumble seat and using the roof. They were usually painted yellow and were thus known as 'yellow bounders'. Both vehicles were of the coupé type, seating two passengers facing forward.

The britzska

Originally an open passenger wagon of Poland and eastern Europe, the britzska developed in Austria and Hungary as a semi-open travelling carriage for two or more people. A version of the Austrian type came to Britain shortly after the Napoleonic Wars, reaching its height of popularity during the 1820s. Its bodywork had a flat-bottomed extension so that passengers might recline at full length, as if in a sleeping compartment, a windscreen or front panel fitting against the half-hood. Some later types also had a semi-enclosed rumble seat for carriage servants. Hung on 'C' springs, supplemented by elliptical springs, a strong underperch joined fore and rear carriages. It was originally driven from a double box seat but later this was removed to provide luggage space and the teams were controlled by postilions. Until the advent of the railways ambassadors and high-ranking diplomats frequently travelled in a britzska, which also carried the diplomatic bag, protected by an

Britzska.

armed escort. Isambard K. Brunel, the engineer and creator of the Great Western Railway system, travelled and slept in a britzska while surveying the main line between Bristol and London.

A slightly smaller but more elegant version of the britzska appeared in France about 1820 and was known as the 'dormeuse'.

The fourgon

Strictly neither a coach nor a carriage in any but the more literal sense, the fourgon was frequently used in conjunction with travelling carriages and all forms of long-distance passenger transport. It was a four-

Fourgon.

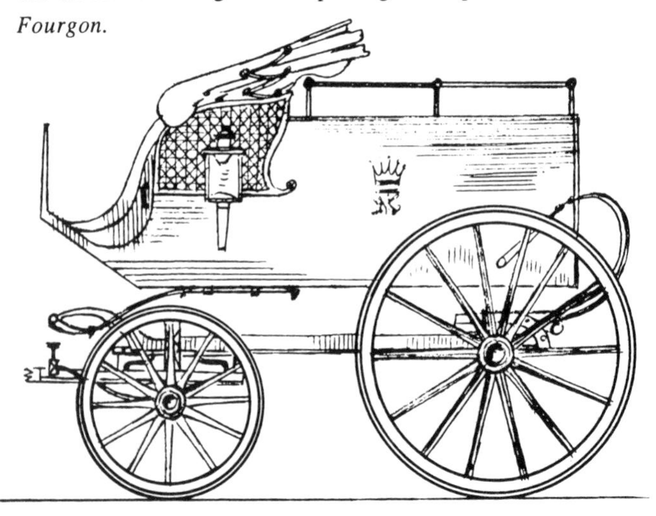

A sociable, built by Silk & Sons, London.

wheeled composite vehicle, having a rearward enclosed compartment for luggage and enlarged crosswise seating under a falling half-hood. It would convey the personal servants of wealthy individuals, travelling ahead of the main party with their essential luggage, to prepare bedrooms in advance. Mounted on combined 'C' and elliptical springs, it was drawn by a pair of swift strong horses in pole gear.

The modern fourgon is a luggage van on a continental passenger train.

The sociable

A semi-open carriage of the mid nineteenth century, sometimes without a box seat, the sociable was controlled from the interior by an owner-driver. Other types were coachman-driven from a box. Four passengers might be seated vis-à-vis, protected by folding hoods. Frequently described as a cross between the barouche and the victoria, it was also known as a 'barouche-sociable'. It was drawn either by a single horse or by a matching pair.

The droshky

A light open or semi-open carriage of Russian origins, the droshky was fashionable in many parts of Europe after the Napoleonic Wars. At first hung on 'C' springs, later versions converted to elliptical or semi-elliptical springs. Fairly low-slung, the passenger seat accommodated two facing forward, being less than 6 inches (150 mm) above the rear axle. A larger version, known in Russia as the *lineika*, seated four passengers vis-à-vis. Both types had falling half-hoods. In Britain the

A Russian droshky given to Queen Victoria by Tsar Nicholas I in 1850, and now in the Tyrwhitt-Drake Museum of Carriages, Maidstone, Kent.

droshky was drawn by a single horse or pair of horses, but in Russia a three-horse team or troika was frequently used. A later refinement of the droshky was the 'pilentum' or low-sided carriage for ladies (a name also used by the ancient Romans), constructed by David Davis, a coachbuilder of Albany Street, London.

The state coach and town coach

Used on formal occasions, the state or dress coach was a large vehicle seating four passengers vis-à-vis. It descended from a box-like conveyance of the Tudor and Stuart periods, used more for prestige and social status than as a means of transport. By the mid eighteenth century it had become widely adopted by those able to afford one, replacing the sedan chair and state (river) barge, especially after the introduction of metal springs and improved road surfaces. State coaches were noted for their fringed, richly embroidered hammercloths and silver candle lamps fitted at each corner of the bodywork. Door panels would be painted with a full coat of arms. Other features included adequate droplights or windows; some coaches had transparent glass panels in place of opaque (solid) upper quarters and were thus known as 'glass coaches'. Footmen usually perched on a rearward dummy board, descending to lower steps, to open doors and to clear the way in crowded places. These coaches were mounted on the arrangement of elbow, 'C' or elliptical springs appropriate to the period. Furnished with a strong underperch, this was perhaps the most impressive of all horse-drawn road vehicles.

State coach.

Town coaches were almost identical with state coaches but less elaborate and in daily use for less formal occasions. They were usually drawn by a well-matched pair of bay horses.

The state or dress chariot

A smaller or coupé version of the state coach, the state chariot seated two passengers facing forward behind a fixed glass panel or windscreen. Like the state and town coach, it had a rearward dummy board and fringed hammercloth. It was not widely used for full-dress occasions until the 1800s. A few state coaches and chariots, with full underperches and turtle-backed boots, were still being made and used into the Edwardian era, mainly appearing at court functions and state occasions.

Dress chariot.

The brougham

A small closed vehicle of the 1830s, the brougham remained popular, as an informal conveyance, for three-quarters of a century. Originally

A dress chariot (c.1860) bearing the arms of the Earl of Yarborough of Brocklesby Park. It was used mainly in London as a court carriage and is now in store at the Museum of Transport in Hull.

A brougham formerly displayed in a collection at Bath.

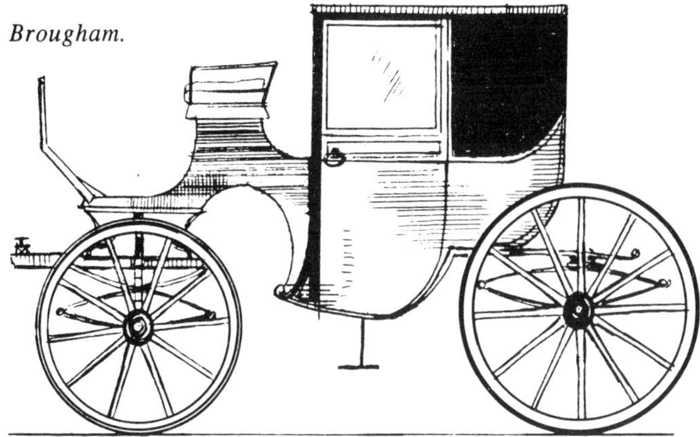
Brougham.

designed as a coupé, with a seat for two passengers facing forward, as in a chariot or half coach, it was the idea of Lord Brougham. It combined the comfort of a coach with the practical advantages of a cab, being cheap to maintain and requiring less space in traffic than a larger vehicle. The box seat was not isolated or detached, as was the case with many coaches and chariots, but formed part of the same structure. It was mounted on elliptical leaf springs. A later type of the 1880s had a bowed rather than a straight forepart of the bodywork and was known as the 'bow-fronted brougham'. Most broughams were drawn by a single horse in shafts, but a larger or 'double brougham' might have vis-à-vis seating and be drawn by a pair of horses in pole gear. Towards the end of the nineteenth century there were two main types in everyday use, the angular 'Peter's brougham' and the rounded, more elegant 'Barker brougham'.

The clarence

A modest family coach, usually drawn by a single horse, the clarence did not have a detached foreboot, box or hammercloth. It seated four passengers vis-à-vis, being larger and more cumbersome than the brougham. Some clarences even had a luggage rack at roof level. In later years many were converted to cabs for public hire. Mounted on elliptical leaf springs and introduced by the firm of Laurie & Marner of Oxford Street, London, in 1842, the clarence was named after the Duke of Clarence, who owned several. A more elaborate version of the clarence, known as the 'sovereign', was produced by Laurie & Marner at a slightly later period.

The victoria

This was long considered one of the most attractive of all open and semi-open carriages. It evolved about 1860, although it was claimed to

A clarence could seat four passengers.

descend from a vehicle used in Paris at least 25 years earlier, known as a 'milord'. This had been greatly admired by the then Prince of Wales and adapted for the use of his mother, Queen Victoria, after whom an updated version was named. It had no connection with an earlier so-called 'victoria', which had been a pony phaeton, its prototype presented to the Queen by a loyal admirer several years before her accession.

As with the brougham, there were both square (angular) and rounded versions; the latter had better lines and was considered more elegant. There were neither doors nor enclosed (upper) side panels (quarters) and the falling or half-hood was seldom raised. Fairly low and easy to enter, especially for ladies with flowing dresses, which its open structure

Victoria.

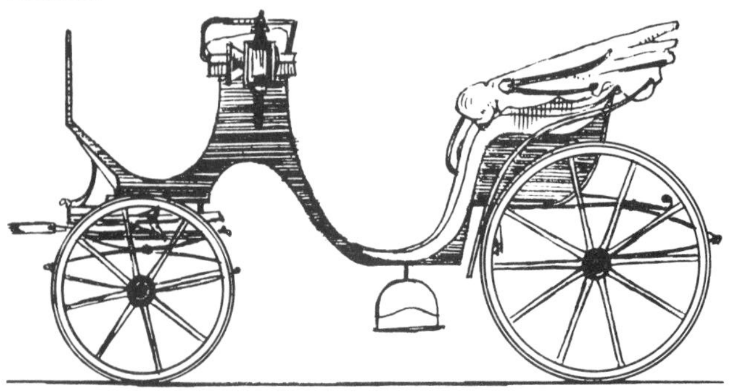

helped to display, it was essentially a vehicle for pleasure driving. It normally carried two passengers facing forward, although a later or 'double victoria' had seats for two extra passengers vis-à-vis. The 'panel boot victoria' had a similar plan, but with folding seats. The 'grand victoria' featured a rumble seat for two footmen. Suspension was based on elliptical and semi-elliptical leaf springs.

The private omnibus

A vehicle, like the fourgon, for both passengers and luggage, the private omnibus was widely used throughout the Victorian era to convey guests of country houses and hotels to and from the railway station. A more elegant version, with fine upholstery, was known as the 'opera bus', used by small parties attending operas, concerts and theatrical performances. Large numbers were also owned or hired by the main-line railway companies and were known as 'station buses'.

Introduced about 1870, the private omnibus remained popular in some districts until the 1920s. Driven from a double seat, raised on curved irons or brackets, directly above the forecarriage, such buses were furnished with an angled footboard and vertical dashboard. Many had a crosswise seat at roof level, to the rear of but slightly higher than the driving seat. Such seats were known as Gammon boards after the member of Parliament who introduced them. Most of the roof area would be occupied by a luggage rack. Private omnibuses were drawn by

The victoria carried two passengers facing forward.

A private omnibus in the Mossman Collection, Luton, Bedfordshire. It is painted in the livery of the 'Favorite'.

a single horse or pair of horses according to size.

Interior seating, approached through a rear door over folding steps, was longitudinal, passengers facing inwards, three on each side. Buses in private ownership had many refinements, with Venetian blinds and button-backed upholstery of quilted satin. One of the smaller versions, with shafts, now on show at the National Railway Museum, York, belonged to the Kent & East Sussex Railway Company, based at Tenterden station.

Private omnibus.

5
Public conveyances

The hackney coach

The name of this vehicle derives from the French word *haquenée*, meaning a work-worn draught horse. There were vehicles of this type plying for hire in both London and Paris throughout the seventeenth and eighteenth centuries. Most were discarded town coaches of the wealthier classes, patched up for a few years of public service before passing to the scrap heap. From the mid seventeenth century they were numerous enough to cause traffic problems, especially in the narrow streets of London before the Great Fire of 1666. They were far from being standard types, either full coach or coupé, drawn by either one or two horses, but mainly by a pair in pole gear. Most were driven from the box but some had a mounted driver or postilion. Ownership of such vehicles eventually came under legal supervision, with rules concerning numbers in use and general safety measures. They continued to provide a service, mainly for the middle and professional classes, until replaced by purpose-built vehicles during the 1790s and 1800s.

The brouette

Although not classed as a horse-drawn vehicle, the brouette represents an important stage in the development of public transport. A French invention of 1668, it was a type of sedan chair on two wheels, for a single passenger only. It would be drawn by a man between shafts, in the style of an oriental rickshaw. A slightly later version, known in England as the 'sedan cart', seated either one or two passengers and was drawn by a pony driven on foot from the gutter with long reins. It was usually unsprung or dead-axle.

The stage-coach

Versions of this vehicle date back to Roman times. They were found in most parts of Europe where there were suitable roads. In Britain they ran between larger towns and centres of population, from the late sixteenth to the mid nineteenth century. They began as crudely enlarged versions of the private travelling coach, and it was nearly two centuries before they came to resemble the stage-coach seen in Christmas cards and picture books. From the late eighteenth century they ran in competition with mail coaches, considered a cheaper but perhaps less efficient alternative, at least until the 1800s. At first unsprung or dead-axle, they were later made with slings or thoroughbraces and finally laminated metal suspension. Telegraph springs, or a combination of crosswise and lengthwise semi-elliptical springs, named after the 'Telegraph' coach first using them, appeared during the early 1800s. Drawn by four or more

The 'Old Times' stage-coach which ran between Chester and Shrewsbury during the nineteenth century. It is now at the Birmingham Museum and Art Gallery.

horses (an extra pair or single was frequently added in steep places), stage-coaches were driven from a box seat forming part of the structural bodywork. The main passenger or inner compartment seated four people, vis-à-vis, while others stood or crouched in a basketwork rumble between the rear wheels. Roof seats, or Gammon boards, were introduced during the early nineteenth century, eventually seating up to fourteen outside passengers. Only four outside passengers were allowed on mail coaches, which may have partly accounted for higher fares on this more exclusive service. Most stage-coaches also carried large amounts of luggage and parcels in ample boots underneath or at the rear. Some parcels and other items such as game birds and turkeys were frequently hung on lamp brackets.

Stage-coaches were usually painted in bright, contrasting colours, having names and destinations emblazoned in large letters. Many had fanciful names such as 'Comet', 'Red Rover', 'Telegraph' and 'Experiment', relating to the routes over which they ran or the inns they served. The majority were owned by large companies or coaching magnates, the two best-known being Chaplin & Horne and Sherman & Company. Smaller versions of the stage-coach, drawn by a pair of horses, provided a feeder service between remote villages or outer suburbs and posting inns on the main routes. Night coaches, drawn by inferior horses, some disfigured by accidents or poor conformation, ran at cheaper rates.

Driving a four-in-hand team, especially to a stage-coach, became the ambition of every schoolboy. The professional coachman was for many years 'king of the road', tipped and treated by his passengers, frequently bribed by young bloods to allow them a few minutes with the 'ribbons' (reins). A seat next to the coachman was always considered a place of honour. Although a slightly less glamorous figure, the guard was in charge of the coach, trained to replace the driver if he became unfit and also expected to summon help from the next inn or village (riding ahead on a detached coach horse) if the need arose. He normally shared a cross-seat with one or two other passengers at the rear of the coach, sounding warning notes on his horn. He also played tunes on a key bugle to amuse the outside passengers, being responsible for their safety and for every package and parcel recorded in the waybill. Like the mail-coach guard, he carried a special clock in a leather pouch and was skilled in the use of firearms.

Horses were changed at inns and posting houses between 7 and 10 miles (11-16 km) apart, according to gradients. Some of these inns served several coaches and also hired out postchaises, with upwards of four hundred horses in their large stables. Crowds thronged inn yards to witness the arrival and departure of their favourite coaches, especially in the London area. The best teams used were on the first stage out, decked with flowers and ribbons on May Day or to celebrate a great victory, such as Trafalgar.

A stage-coach in action at a county show.

While lever brakes were fitted to most later coaches, the majority of coachmen scorned to use them, unless the vehicle was at a standstill. Some coachmen used the drag shoe only, although even this was ignored by more skilful drivers.

The stage wagon

This may be termed the 'poor man's stage-coach'. Slow, safe and unlikely to overturn, it carried not only passengers but boxes and bales of merchandise, between which the human cargo had to squeeze, although they were forced to dismount on rising gradients. The chief danger was from fire, started by overheated axles (when greasing had been neglected) or by hot ashes from a passenger's pipe catching tinder-dry canvas.

The average panel-sided road wagon had, at least from the mid seventeenth century, well-dished wheels with broad, iron-straked treads that helped to flatten lumps and ruts for other traffic. A cover of thick canvas was stretched from end to end of the bodywork, supported by hoops or tilts. A large team of heavy horses, sometimes a dozen or more, was controlled by a wagoner who either walked alongside with a cart whip or rode a nimble pony. Unlike stage-coaches, stage wagons were seldom robbed by highwaymen as they were rarely patronised by wealthy passengers.

The mail coach

Perhaps the best-known and most romantic of all public transport vehicles, the mail coach was introduced by John Palmer of Bath in 1784 as a stage-coach adapted to carry the Royal Mail, replacing an unreliable service of mounted postboys. The first official service ran between

Mail coach.

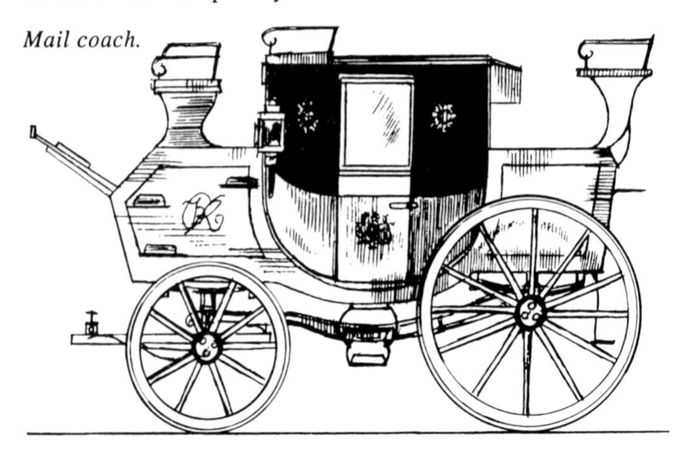

The London to Exeter mail coach, 1843, from Fore's 'Coaching Recollections'.

London and Bristol. By 1807 its range had extended as far north as Berwick-on-Tweed and the Scottish Lowlands, west to Penzance and east to Great Yarmouth. In Wales the mail coach reached Holyhead in the north and Milford Haven in the south-west, with routes through central Wales to Newtown and Aberystwyth. Key centres such as York, Shrewsbury, Oxford, Exeter, Canterbury and Birmingham were at the junction of several routes; all services radiated from London.

Mail coaches were hired by the government and were constructed to strict specifications by the firm of John Vidler & Company of Millbank, London. They were painted in the royal livery of scarlet, maroon and black, with royal arms on the door panels, a royal cipher on the foreboot and stars of the senior orders of chivalry on the four upper quarters. The guard-in-charge wore a scarlet and gold livery, sitting on a single, rearmost seat, with the mail bags in a locker under his feet. He would be armed to protect the coach with cutlass, blunderbuss and a brace of loaded pistols. The coach horn was carried in a leather case, while that of the stage-coach guard may have been of basketwork. He sounded his horn so that ostlers at the next post house might prepare a change of horses and tollkeepers could open their gates, through which mail coaches passed without stopping. Nothing was allowed to hinder the mail coach, which scattered pedestrians and even herds of cattle in busy market towns if they should appear to block the highway. Mail guards were not allowed to play tunes on key bugles or any other instrument and unnecessary conversation was discouraged. The timekeeping of mail coaches and of many stage-coaches was so accurate that houses on the main roads set their clocks by them.

The first 'Palmer' coach was very similar to a family travelling coach of the period, apart from its livery. It would be mounted fairly high on elbow springs, but later there were sets of two-way Telegraph springs at both front and rear. With early types the driver and guard shared the same box seat and no outside passengers were allowed. There would be a strongly reinforced underperch supporting the main bodywork. The passenger compartment, mounted in the centre of a shell-like structure that also enclosed the luggage and mail boots, eventually supported the driving seat and a rearward guard's seat mounted on brackets. In its later form the box seat, with angled footboard, was in two sections divided by side irons. The driver's portion was unpadded, lest he should be too comfortable, fall asleep and lose control of the horses. The forward passenger seat, however, was well upholstered. There was a three-aspect lamp fitted to the centre-front of the footboard, and there were two headlamps and two slightly smaller side lamps placed above wheel level on either side of the forebody.

The four-in-hand team would be driven at an average speed of $10^{1}/_{4}$ miles (16.5 km) per hour. The only named mail coach, running between London and Falmouth, was known as 'Quick Silver'. It covered the 176 miles (283 km) to Exeter in sixteen hours, allowing time for meals, change of horses and post-office business.

The touring coach

This vehicle was in many ways similar to the stage or mail coach, sometimes converted from a 'road' coach in regular service. Later examples were purpose-built, being less elegant than their predecessors. The average touring coach was of a compact solid construction, its forewheels small enough to turn in half lock. Roof seats were much higher than those of the conventional stage-coach, all facing forward for better sightseeing and on a slightly higher level than the driver. Although the coach had mail-coach hubs and axles, the proportions of the wheels and general structure resembled those of a cart or wagon rather than an élite passenger vehicle.

Coaching tours, lasting from a few hours to a whole day, were mainly popular from the 1880s to the First World War, although continuing in some parts until the 1930s. The main centres were picturesque parts of Scotland, north Wales, the Lake District and the west of England (especially Exmoor). Both Llandudno and Colwyn Bay were important centres for regular trips of up to 56 miles (90 km) through Snowdonia, taking about seven and a half hours, with frequent changes and a midday lunch break at Betws-y-coed. Some of the later Llandudno coaches were so popular that they were converted from fourteen to twenty-two seaters,

A private road coach resting en route to a county show.

excluding coachman and guard. Some coaches were known as 'dummies', appearing to have a passenger compartment, but with a roof too low for internal use. At one period several of these vehicles were built and serviced in Llandudno.

Private drags and road coaches

These were private coaches, usually of lighter construction and more elegant than public or 'road' coaches. Designed for the sole use of amateur coachmen or owner-drivers, they ran frequently on estate or private roads but took part in marathon drives over public highways. During later years they appeared in special classes at horse shows and took part in events organised by the Coaching Club, while serving as grandstands at fashionable sporting events. Some were owned by regiments or corps of the British Army and were known as 'regimental coaches', the last of which in regular service is owned by the Household Cavalry mounted regiment. Private drags would be turned out in a dark but dignified family livery. Two young grooms of identical height and weight, also wearing family colours, shared the rearmost roof seat. They kept the horses still before starting and ran alongside the team to make sure everything was in order, scrambling aboard at the last moment. They also jumped down to help stop the wheelers as the coach drew to a halt, before the brakes were applied. Stopping the leaders first was not advisable as this might cause the wheelers to pile up from behind and the coach to slew or perhaps overturn. Passengers on private drags were usually friends of the owner-driver or his invited guests. They always travelled on top as the interior of the coach was kept locked and seldom used.

Regular stage-coaches, either purpose-built or modified, are also shown in driving classes at horse shows, competing with private and regimental drags in trial runs or marathons. They are known as 'road' coaches and usually seem more colourful than 'drags', frequently having mixed rather than matching teams. A guard in scarlet livery and top hat replaces the identical footmen. He is also allowed to sound his coach horn, a practice considered incorrect on private coaches.

The coffin cab

This was a two-wheeled cab of the early nineteenth century that resembled an up-ended coffin. Although a few may have been guided on long reins at road level, most had the 'cabbie' perched on a side seat projecting above the offside wheel. A single passenger faced forward and sheltered behind a high leather apron beneath a falling or half-hood. The coffin cab descended directly from the earlier brouette and sedan cart.

The London cab

A later version of the sedan cart or cab and slightly more comfortable than the coffin cab, the London cab was usually cheaper than the hackney coach. Wheels were fairly high and the bodywork of greater breadth than with other types. The half-hood could be lowered in fine weather but was usually kept in the raised position. There was sufficient room for two passengers seated abreast, facing forward.

The American cab

A two-wheeled cab of the 1830s first appearing in the streets of New York, but later reaching London and other centres, the American cab seated four passengers on longitudinal seats, or two each side, facing inwards. It was entered through a rear door by means of a single step iron. The driver was perched on a front seat at roof level.

The Gurney cab and similar types

Introduced about the same time as the American cab, the Gurney cab was considered safer and more comfortable. The interior seating was similar for both vehicles, but the driving position, on brackets, with an angled footboard, would be much lower for better control in the Gurney cab.

The tribus was a three-passenger cab of the 1840s, both entered and driven from the rear. The Boulnois cab or 'mini-bus' had sideways-on seats for two, vis-à-vis. Named after its inventor, it was considered awkward and top-heavy, despite its narrow proportions. What might be termed a third version of the sedan cab appeared much later, having room

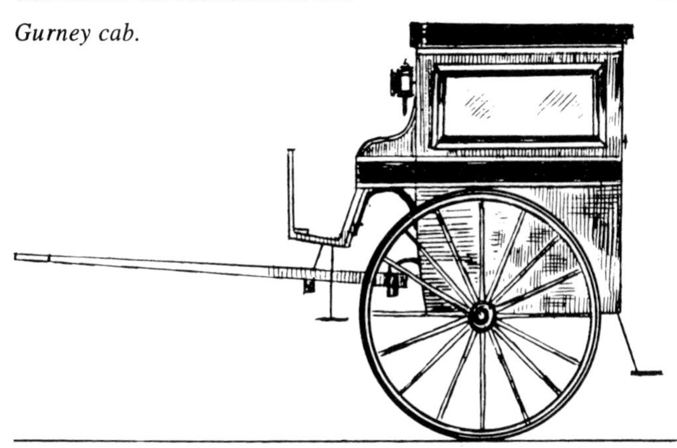
Gurney cab.

for two people on hinged seats lowered from side-panels of the interior.

The hansom cab

The first hansom cab appeared in 1834, named after its inventor. It was designed with two large wheels, higher than roof level, to prevent it overturning at speed, while making draught easier for the horse. The driver first sat on the front part of the roof, as with the American cab. Later versions, lighter but more elegant, introduced by John Chapman in 1836, were to become one of the most popular public transport vehicles of the nineteenth century. The Chapman version had a cranked axle and was driven from the rear of the double passenger compartment, which seated two abreast on well-upholstered cushions of a cross-seat. Passengers entered through the semi-open front, boxed in for safety by hinged

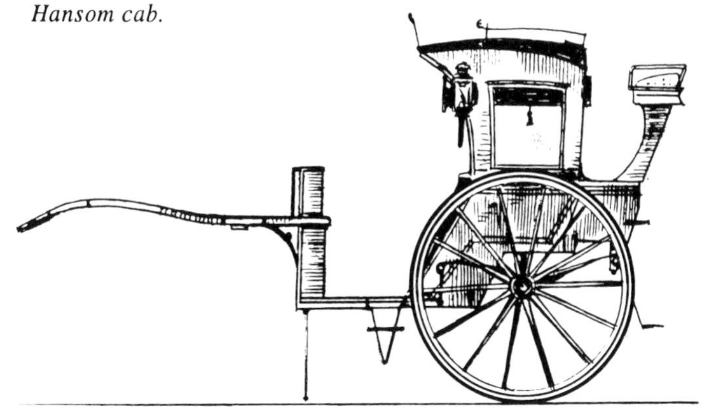
Hansom cab.

A Forder hansom cab of c.1880 in the Mossman Collection, Luton, Bedfordshire.

knee-flaps. An even more refined version, often used as a private vehicle by professional men, was fully enclosed, bow-fronted and entered through a side door with droplights. Both 'C' and elliptical side springs were used.

A bow-fronted hansom cab c.1889, in use in Hull until the early 1920s and now in store at the Hull Museum of Transport.

What might be termed a third and final phase of construction was the Forder hansom of 1873. This was light, swift and reverted to the straight axle. Interiors were fitted out with looking glasses and silver ashtrays, tare weight being only about 8 cwt (406 kg). Large numbers eventually operated on the streets of London and other cities, many owned by the main-line railway companies, especially in the provinces. They were considered fast and dashing, unsuitable for an unescorted female of good reputation. Other variations of the hansom cab were the rear-door or omnibus type and the 'hooded cab' with falling or half-hood for holiday resorts and summer driving. Hansoms greatly outnumbered four-wheelers and other types, although they declined in popularity from the 1890s, mainly owing to improved omnibus services and the arrival of motorised cabs or taxis.

The four-wheeled cab or growler

This vehicle was also known as a 'four-wheeler'. Descended from the hackney coach via the clarence and double brougham, it was large enough for at least four adults and two or three small children, with luggage stowed in a roof rack. It was driven to a single horse in shafts, with a box seat and angled footboard directly above the forecarriage, and was mounted on elliptical leaf springs. While hansoms appealed to the young and fashionable, four-wheelers were more suitable for staid, elderly people or families. Drivers of four-wheelers were frequently of greater maturity than those of hansom cabs; some of the latter were driven as a hobby by young men with independent means. Horses in the shafts of a hansom were usually of good quality while those drawing four-wheeled cabs might be broken creatures one remove from the street markets and knacker's yard.

Growler.

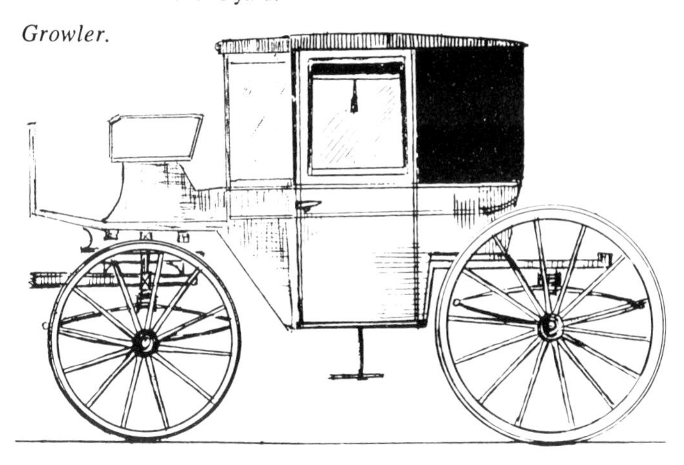

A growler formerly displayed in Bath.

The omnibus

George Shillibeer introduced the omnibus from Paris to London in 1829. His intention was to provide an alternative to hackney coaches and short stage-coaches, which he hoped might prove more comfortable but less expensive. He went into business with two single-deckers which ran between Paddington and the Bank of England, a route already covered by short stage-coaches and later by the patent steam carriages of Walter Hancock. Each bus was drawn by three bay horses, harnessed abreast. Drivers and conductors, unlike many hackney coachmen and cabbies, were sober, polite and dressed in smart uniforms. The latest newspapers were always available free of charge and, for a short period (until many of the books were stolen), a lending library. Unfortunately three horses abreast, in the French or Russian style, were said to be difficult to control and took up too much room on busy streets. When the Metropolitan Police Force was founded three-horse buses were banned from public service and Shillibeer was forced to rely on smaller buses, each drawn by a pair. The original service ran twelve return journeys each day, making reasonable profits. Omnibuses soon became popular and many rival firms sprang up, so that Shillibeer eventually withdrew his interest, ending his career as an undertaker and also inventing a patent hearse named after him.

The next important development was the so-called 'knifeboard' omnibus, a double-decker of the 1850s with back-to-back roof seats on the longitudinal plan, reached by a near-vertical ladder. It needed great agility to mount the upper deck, impossible for elderly people, young children or women with hampering dresses. Inside passengers entered through the rear and sat facing inwards on either side of a central gangway. Suspension was in the form of both lengthwise and crosswise elliptical springs.

A great improvement on the knifeboard was the 'garden-seat bus', which had longitudinal inner seating with a double row of forward-facing seats on the upper deck. This vehicle type remained popular until motor buses took over shortly before the First World War. During the 1900s there were over four thousand garden-seat buses working in the London area alone. Among their improved features were safer steps to the upper deck, guarded by a hand rail, and the addition of decency boards to screen the lower limbs and petticoats of women passengers. The driver sat fairly high on a single seat, with an angled footboard bracketed to the front of the vehicle. Most buses were plastered with advertisements for branded goods, giving them a distinctly commercial

A knifeboard omnibus in London in 1891.

A garden-seat omnibus in London about 1890.

appearance. By the 1880s a small rear step for the conductor had been replaced by the larger and more familiar platform. Garden-seat buses ran from 1881 to 1914, although they were discarded by the London General Omnibus Company in 1911. Horses for both knifeboard and garden-seat types would be a pair in pole gear, usually mares and frequently imported from Ireland.

6
Owner-driven passenger vehicles

Some of the most typical vehicles of this category began to appear during the second half of the eighteenth century. This marked the beginning of a new era when driving ceased to be a chore and became an increasingly popular leisure pursuit.

From the 1780s privately owned and driven four-wheeled vehicles were known as 'phaetons'. In classical legend Phaeton was the son of Helios, driver of the sun chariot. An impetuous youth, he begged permission to drive the sun but lost control of his team, destroying the universe in the ensuing crash, which symbolised nightfall. The drivers of the carriages named after him were thought to have a reckless attitude similar to that of Phaeton.

Some types in this category were driven by professional coachmen, although on informal occasions not requiring full dress or formal livery.

The continental chaise

Introduced about 1760, the continental chaise descended from the Italian *carretta* or pleasure cart, drawn by a pony or mule. A comparatively light vehicle for its day, it was popular in both France and England until the French Revolution. The single driving seat and low dashboard were suspended above a shallow framework on toughened leather braces. The English version was stronger and perhaps safer. It had smaller wheels and higher sides, but its centre of gravity was too low, often straining the back of the horse between the shafts. A shaft step, on both sides, was little more than a metal ring set at an angle of 45 degrees. Shafts were straight rather than curved, especially on earlier models. Sides were ornate with richly carved and painted surfaces. A similar vehicle of this period, surviving in country districts of Holland, was the

Continental chaise.

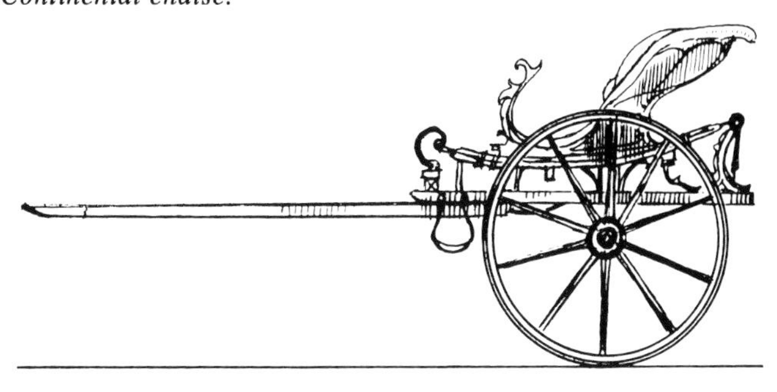

Frisian sjees.

'Frisian sjees', although some were drawn by a pair in pole gear. Curved lines and inset panels reflected rococo styles in furnishing and architecture.

A continental chaise exhibited at Windsor in 1939.

Crane-necked phaeton.

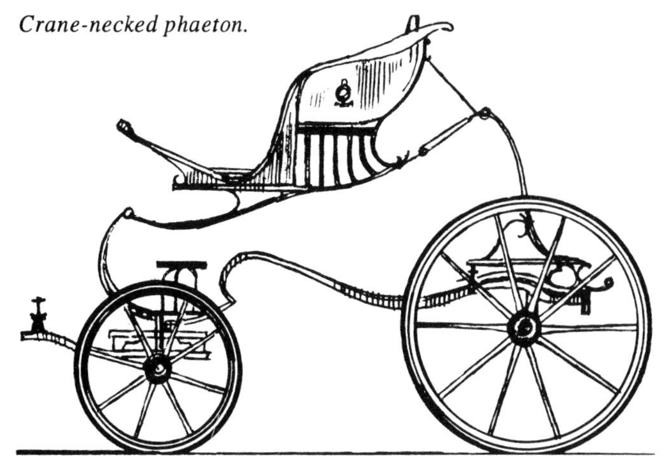

The crane-necked phaeton

This was an essentially sporting vehicle of the 1780s, used for driving with a turn of speed and a taste of danger. It was four-wheeled with a seat for two mounted some distance above ground level. While an earlier version appeared with a heavy underperch and smaller wheels, the more popular type had near-vertical curved iron supports or 'cranes' under which larger forewheels turned in improved lock; its lighter perch was also raised above the fore-end. This was a dangerous, unstable design, especially for fast work with a pair of horses or larger team. Front wheels of the later type were 5 feet (1.5 metres) in diameter while back wheels were up to 8 feet (2.4 metres), although usually 6 feet (1.8 metres). Both types were known as 'high-flyers', a nickname also given to the daring young men and occasionally young women by whom they were driven. Perhaps the best-known female driver or 'whip' of the period was the notorious Lady Archer, 'as renowned for her skill with the whip as for the cosmetic powers she exercised on her complexion'. Lady Lade was another, even more formidable Amazon of this fast set.

The crane-necked phaeton was a popular mode of transport for the Prince of Wales (later Prince Regent and George IV) and his circle. They would be driven to singles, pairs or even four-in-hand teams. Some attempted to hitch sixes, but this proved impractical even for park driving. With any team of four or more a postilion would ride the nearside leader. Suspension appeared in the form of whip springs. Most phaetons had a rearward dummy board for the groom.

The high cocking cart

A two-wheeled sporting vehicle for a driver and single passenger side by side, the high cocking cart, in some aspects, resembled the detached front half of a stage-coach. It came into vogue during the late 1790s, shortly after the crane-necked phaeton. The high driving seat was raised above a compartment with slatted sides in which fighting cocks were taken to a match or 'main'. It was driven either to a single horse or a tandem pair, often at break-neck speed. A version of the cocking cart native to Ireland was the 'suicide gig', which had an even higher driving seat and a rear seat for the groom. Even mounting this vehicle was to risk life and limb.

High cocking cart.

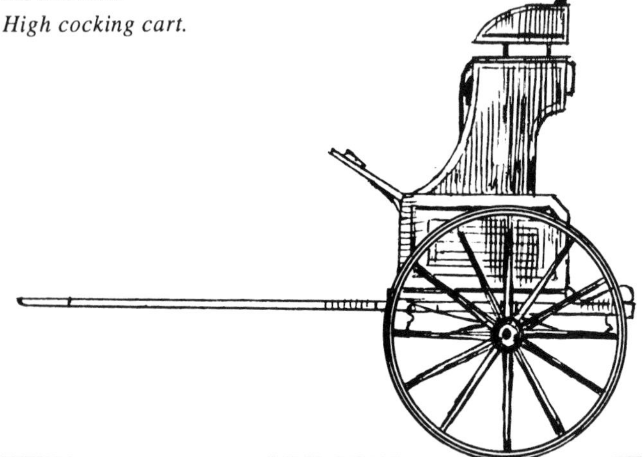

The curricle

The curricle, as both a two-wheeled carriage and a style of driving gear, derived from the chariots of antiquity, reintroduced in Italy during the second half of the eighteenth century. It became popular in England from the 1800s, especially under the patronage of the Prince Regent. It was half-hooded and comparatively low-slung, having a rearward rumble seat for a diminutive groom known as a 'tiger', the latter so-named as he wore a striped livery. Drawn by a steady, level-stepping pair, the curricle had a reputation for being smart and swift but easy to control. Suspension was in the form of 'C' springs. Frequently driven by the Duke of Wellington, among other notables, the curricle remained popular for about forty years. It was also revived towards the end of the nineteenth century, when some were fitted with rubber tyres.

The cabriolet

This appeared during the second decade of the nineteenth century and at one time threatened the popularity of the curricle. Like that vehicle it

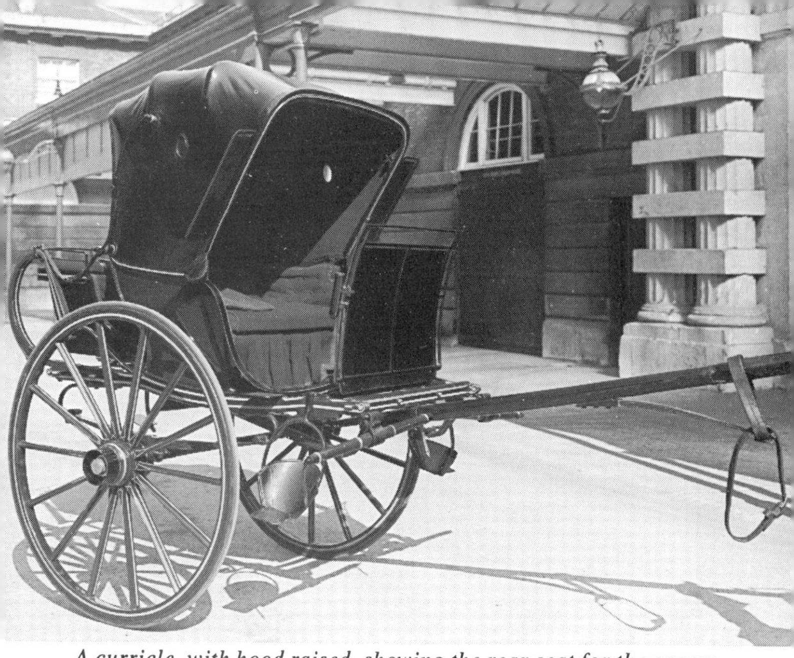

A curricle, with hood raised, showing the rear seat for the groom or 'tiger'.

This curricle, fitted with pneumatic tyres, was photographed in use c.1900.

Cabriolet.

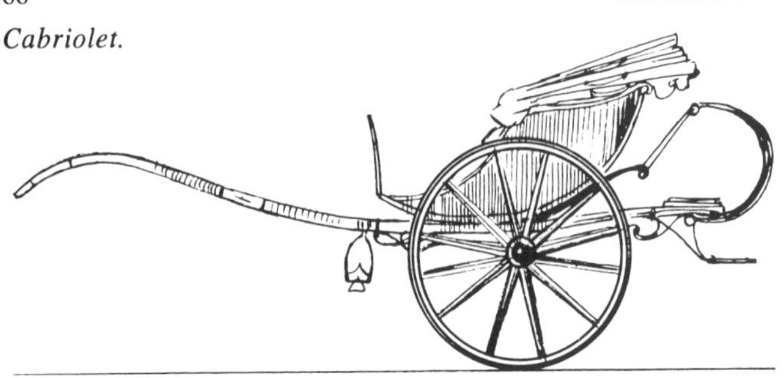

was a two-wheeled carriage in the more conservative sense of these words, sporting a half-hood and suspended on 'C' springs. Among its sponsors were Charles Dickens and an expatriate French nobleman, the Comte d'Orsay, last of the dandies. It was fashionable to drive a tall powerful horse of the thoroughbred type, cared for by a dwarfish groom or 'tiger' who rode the dummy board in a standing position. The vehicle being low-slung, the shafts were curved upwards at the fore-end rather than straight. As cabriolets were normally driven at a fast pace, the harness included a warning bell of a type later carried by hansom cabs.

A cabriolet c.1820 bearing the arms of the Goldsmid family.

Caned whisky.

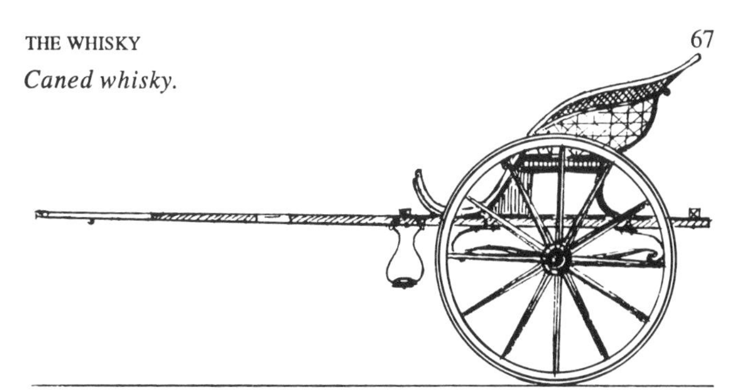

The whisky

Introduced about 1812, this was a two-wheeled gig-like vehicle, perhaps descended from the continental chaise, drawn by a small horse or large pony, and used for short journeys at high speed. The shell-shaped body was mounted on a framework of flexible shafts that formed an essential part of its suspension. A single crossbar usually enclosed the forepart as a foot rest. Exterior bodywork was of woven canework, accounting for the alternative name of 'caned whisky'. Long before whisky was accepted as a fashionable drink for upper-class people, the name derived from the way in which the vehicle 'whisked' over the ground. A slightly smaller and even lighter version was known as the 'grasshopper whisky'.

The Dennet gig

At one period the name 'gig' was frequently bestowed on any cheap, two-wheeled vehicle, owner-driven by those unable to afford anything better. 'Gig' in this case was a contraction of 'whirligig', meaning something superficial and of inferior worth. If such a vehicle cost less than £12 to make it was taxed very low, at only a few shillings *per annum*,

Plain gig (1820).

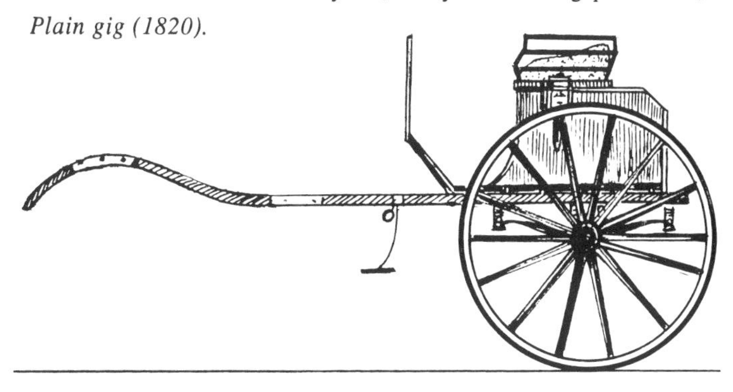

but had to be painted with the humiliating slogan 'tax cart'. During the early nineteenth century the design and quality of gigs began to improve, especially for sporting purposes. The Dennet gig was in the 'improved' category, suitable for driving in either town or country. Like all gigs, it was enclosed at the rear but with a luggage space or 'buck' under the driving seat. It was named after three fashionable sisters, also stage dancers, about 1814. Its main feature was a unique system of three-spring suspension, each of two lengthwise springs and one cross-spring named after a sister.

The Stanhope gig

Introduced about 1816, this was also a superior type of vehicle, constructed by a coachbuilder named Tilbury to designs by the Honourable Fitzroy Stanhope, a noted amateur whip of the period. It hung on two lengthwise and two crosswise springs, sometimes having a rarely used rearward (folding) half-hood. The driving seat was in the form of a rib-backed chair. It was much heavier than the Dennet gig.

Stanhope gig.

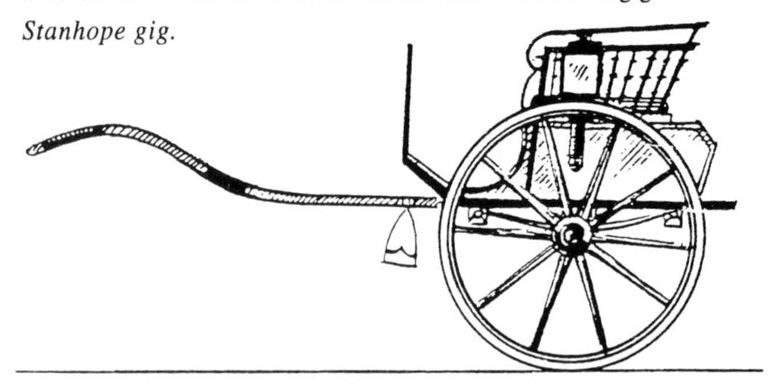

The tilbury

Made by Tilbury of London, responsible for the Stanhope gig and several other light vehicles of this era, the tilbury was one of the most popular two-wheelers in Europe during the first half of the nineteenth century, especially in Spain, Italy and Portugal. Mounted on six undersprings, it could negotiate some of the roughest and steepest roads in any part of the continent. It was also considered one of the heaviest gigs on account of the ironwork used in its suspension. The driving seat was rib-backed. Many appeared open and without a half-hood.

The Lawton gig and the Liverpool gig

The Lawton and Liverpool gigs were very much the same types of vehicle, introduced about 1860. Lawton ran a firm of carriage builders in Liverpool, his native city, and he was the designer and builder of the

A Stanhope gig.

A tilbury.

superior gigs named after him. Liverpool gigs were, for the most part, either by or in the style of Lawton, although some were eventually constructed in other centres. Recognised for many years as the acme of their type, all featured a straight back rest or rail, a high dashboard and

A Liverpool gig.

upward curving shafts, with 'splashers' or mudguards.

The English buggy

The original buggy was a two-wheeled vehicle, fairly low-slung and related to a version of the cabriolet. Mounted on shallow, half-elliptical or platform springs, fitting longitudinally beneath a curved underbody, it dated from the early nineteenth century but was revived about forty years later. Most had a covered double driving seat and were known as 'headed' or 'hooded' buggies. Some had a rearward groom's seat or rumble. The 'Duke of York's buggy' was slightly larger and higher above ground level than its counterparts and was made by Lawton & Goodman of London. Frequently without its half-hood, it was a swift sporting vehicle of combined lightness and strength, favoured by Lord Lonsdale in his epic race against time, for a wager, in 1891. The 'Connaught buggy' was a smaller, hooded type, suitable for lady drivers, and designed for HRH the Duchess of Connaught. She drove it mainly in India.

The sulky

This type of vehicle has been in use from the 1800s to the present day, although modern versions have greatly changed in appearance. An extremely light, two-wheeled vehicle (in its original form), driven solo without passenger or groom, it was considered anti-social. Widely used in training and showing light harness horses or ponies, it was later

Hooded buggy c.1880.

adapted for trotting matches. The original sulky had two large wheels, its suspension depending on highly flexible shafts and undercarriage. The modern type is much smaller, with wire-spoked, rubber-shod 'bicycle' wheels. A four-wheeled twentieth-century version, used almost exclusively for showing hackney ponies, is known in England as the 'Mills wagon'.

The pony phaeton

Phaetons, introduced during the late eighteenth century, declined in popularity from the 1800s, to be revived, often in smaller versions, about twelve to fifteen years later. One of the later type was a pony phaeton favoured by George IV, forsaking his 'high-flyers' and curricles for a more sedate form of transport. The advantage of the pony phaeton, especially for the elderly or lady drivers with flowing dresses, was its low bodywork; it was driven from the interior and reached by a step iron only a few inches above ground level. Wheel tops were protected by 'splashers'

A George IV phaeton.

or mudguards; the front wheels were a mere 20 inches (500 mm) in diameter and the rear ones 30 inches (760 mm). Such vehicles usually had a folding half-hood and protective leather apron.

A small 'basketwork phaeton' was introduced for driving children, especially in parks and over private estate roads. This was safe and easy to enter for even the smallest child and had few exposed areas of paintwork for grubby fingers to smear or scratch. When driven by ladies the pony phaeton was frequently escorted by a mounted groom, but some also acquired a rearward groom's seat or rumble. The 'park phaeton' of 1834 would be hitched to a pair in pole gear but was restricted to fine-weather driving, usually lacking a hood or apron. All types were mounted on elliptical springs, front and rear.

The mail phaeton

A new era for the larger type of phaeton dawned during the 1830s, one of its most characteristic examples being the mail phaeton. This closely resembled the front half of a mail coach, not unlike the earlier cocking cart, but running on four wheels, and it was suitable only for an experienced and physically strong driver. It was sometimes used to convey mails and parcels in remote areas (carried in an underboot), but mainly to exercise and train a pair of coach horses. The horses would be harnessed in chain rather than leather traces. The driving seat had a falling or half-hood, while the groom's seat or rumble would be open. As the rear seat was boxed in, access to it was through crescent-shaped side doors, so designed to avoid catching the rear wheels. The 'Beaufort mail

Mail phaeton.

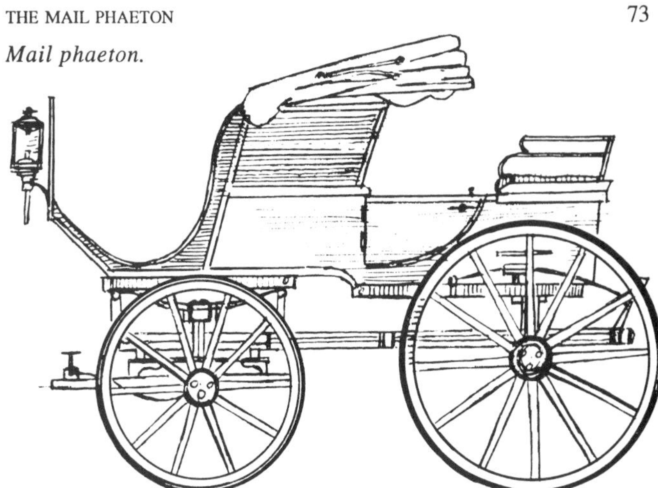

phaeton' was an even larger version, but on the same lines, able to seat five.

The demi-mail phaeton

Much smaller and lighter than the mail phaeton, the demi-mail phaeton seated three persons, including a groom. The driving seat was

A mail phaeton in the Tyrwhitt-Drake Museum of Carriages, Maidstone, Kent.

A demi-mail phaeton formerly exhibited in Bath.

rib-backed. This vehicle was considered more elegant and easier to control than the mail phaeton and was thus frequently driven by ladies in parks and at fashionable resorts. It usually had a hood that was kept in a raised position.

The Stanhope phaeton

Another popular vehicle designed by the Honourable Fitzroy Stanhope and constructed by Tilbury, the Stanhope phaeton was introduced about 1830. It was lighter even than the demi-mail phaeton and driven to a

Stanhope phaeton.

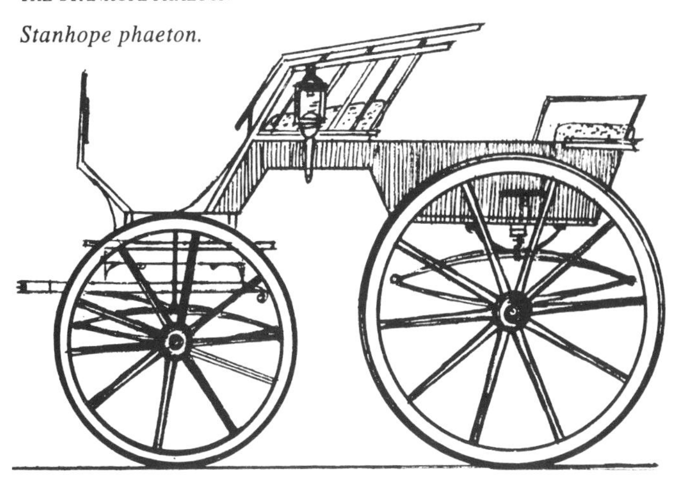

small horse or large pony. It had elliptical springs at both front and rear. It normally seated a driver and passenger at the front, with either one or two grooms in the rumble. The driving seat was rib-backed, appearing either with or without a half-hood. Shafts were attached to open-ended futchells or projections of the undercarriage, to be removed for storage purposes. This was essentially a town or park vehicle.

'T' cart phaeton.

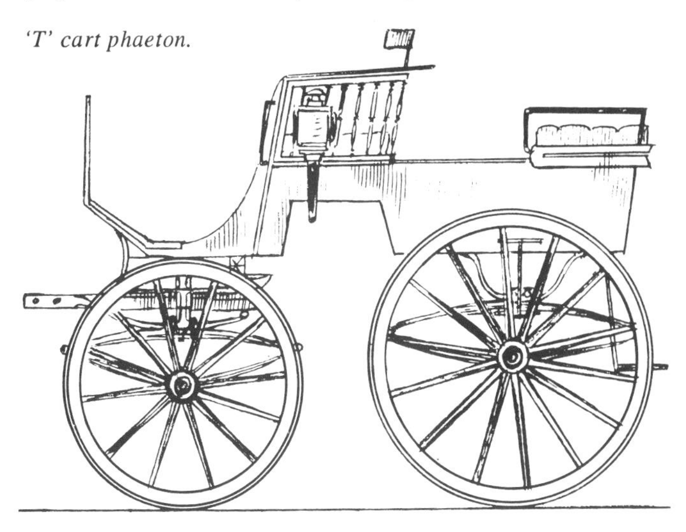

The 'T' cart phaeton

A light phaeton designed by an officer in the foot guards about 1833, the 'T' cart phaeton was fashionable in military circles until the closing decades of the nineteenth century. Similar to the Stanhope phaeton in many features, it was drawn by a small horse or pony not more than 14 hands high. (One hand equals 4 inches or 102 mm, measured from ground level to the top of the withers or shoulders.) The rear seat or rumble was narrower than the driving seat; seen from above, it was T-shaped.

The spider phaeton

An elegant, four-wheeled vehicle of the 1880s that closely resembled the high-flyer of the late eighteenth century, the spider phaeton was said to have a tilbury-type body with a single groom's or rumble seat at the rear. The body was mounted on arched irons for improved underlock, with full elliptical springs front and rear. Often used for park driving and showing the paces of a fast, well-bred horse, this type of phaeton was favoured by Lord Lonsdale during the 1890s and 1900s. The half-hood was usually kept in the lowered position.

Spider phaeton.

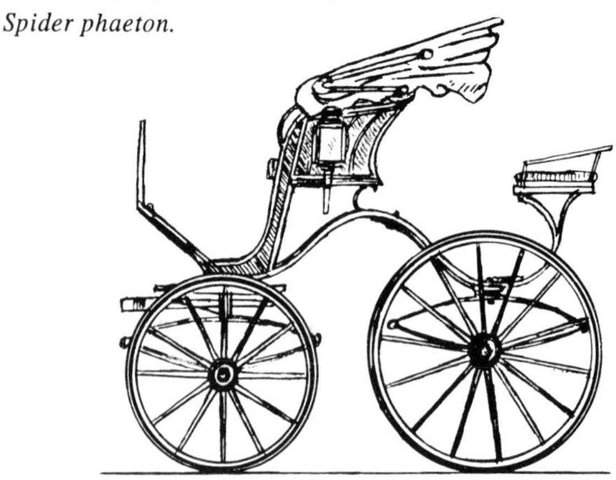

Cars and carts

These were mainly used as country and estate vehicles, appearing in a variety of shapes and sizes and often produced by local or village craftsmen. While the majority of gigs had only two occupants, cars and carts held four or even five people. They were greatly favoured by the farming community and country tradesmen, although sporting farmers frequently drove gigs of the Liverpool-Lawton type.

Dogcart.

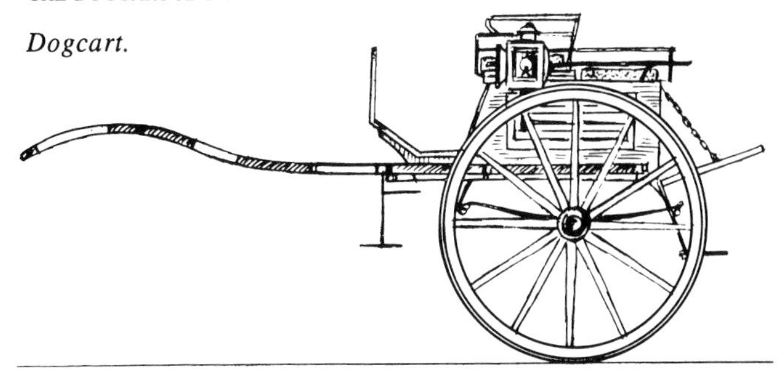

The dogcart and dogcart phaeton

Introduced during the 1800s, these vehicles were used to convey members of a shooting party and their dogs. The ordinary dogcart was two-wheeled, driven to a single horse or pony and available in large and small sizes. The four-wheeled dogcart or dogcart phaeton could be harnessed to a single horse in shafts or a pair in pole gear. Both had a forward driving seat for two and two rearward-facing seats, the passengers sitting back to back or dos-à-dos. The feet of rear passengers were supported by an angled footboard on letting-down chains. Dogs were kept in an underboot with slatted side panels. Shafts were curved upward rather than straight. Like many other country vehicles, dogcarts were exempt from heavy taxes.

The dogcart phaeton descended from a tray-bodied shooting cart or wagon, its suspension based on full elliptical springs front and rear. Two-wheeled dogcarts utilised semi-elliptical or shallow platform springs.

Four-wheeled dogcart (rear spokes removed to show suspension).

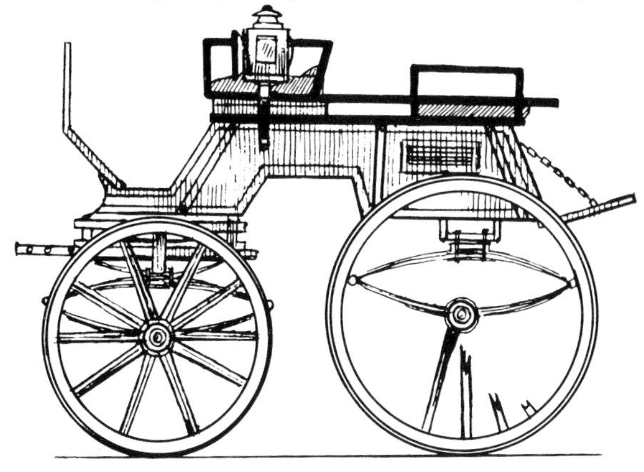

The dogcart phaeton was a popular country and sporting carriage. This one, c.1860, is in store at the Museum of Transport in Hull.

Later versions of both types, some mainly for show purposes, had dummy slats and sliding seats, the latter mounted on runners to improve the driving position. Special two-wheeled dogcarts were used for driving tandem and known as 'tandem carts'. Many vehicles of this type appeared during the second half of the nineteenth century. Most were named after their place of origin such as the 'Malvern cart' and the 'Worcester cart', each having numerous minor differences. Their main feature in common would be back-to-back seating.

The Manchester market cart

There were several regional market carts of much the same type, although the Manchester market cart was the most popular and widely used. A two-wheeled, panel-sided vehicle of the 1870s, it survived well into the twentieth century. Suitable for trade purposes, although a compromise between passenger and goods vehicle, it was favoured by country shopkeepers. In effect it was a cheaper version of the dogcart, with room for market produce in place of the dog compartment. Suspension was in the form of shallow platform or semi-elliptical springs. Shafts were usually straight but less frequently curved, with a low footboard or toeboard in place of an angled footboard and dashboard. Most seated four passengers dos-à-dos. Cost would have been about £12.

A type of dogcart known as a tandem cart, formerly on display in Bath.

The ralli car or cart

Usually known as a 'car', although there has been much controversy on this subject since its introduction in 1898, this vehicle was known in most parts of Wales as a 'rally cart'. Its design featured in an important lawsuit concerning patent rights that was widely reported in the daily press. A correspondent for the *Daily Telegraph* described it as a 'clothes basket', and this became its popular nickname. It was similar to the two-wheeled dogcart, with dos-à-dos seating. The body was lower than that

Manchester market cart.

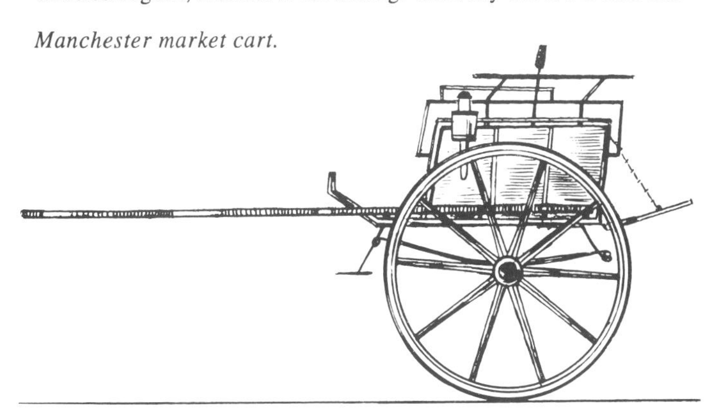

A pony-sized ralli car, built by Windovers of London.

of other similar vehicles, with shafts fitted either inside or outside the bodywork, reducing its height. Most carts had shafts under the main bodywork. Most ralli cars carried four people but an early type seated only two on a single cross-bench with straight back rest. Those used in country districts were stained or varnished rather than painted and were more likely to be known as 'carts'. Sides curved above the wheeltops.

The jaunting car

An open two-wheeled passenger car of Irish origins, drawn by a single horse, the jaunting car is said to descend from the primitive 'trottle car'. Having heavy framework and disc wheels, it first appeared in Ulster during the late eighteenth century and is noted for its back-to-back but sideways-on seating. Two passengers would be seated on either side, facing outwards, sharing a common footboard. The driver sat on an either plain or padded seat, slightly higher than his passengers, with an angled footboard supported on brackets. Suspension was in the form of sideways semi-elliptical leaf springs. Shafts were straight rather than curved. Also known as 'outside cars', 'side cars' or 'jaunties', such vehicles now mainly appear at resorts in the west of Ireland, as a tourist attraction. These are a lighter, improved version on spoked wheels.

During the early nineteenth century an Italian named Bianconi, who lived in Ireland, devised a type of four-wheeled side car that would take

An Irish jaunting car.

fourteen passengers, plus driver and guard. Drawn by either a unicorn or a four-in-hand team, and appearing in country districts on routes not covered by stage-coaches, they were known as 'Bians' and eventually contracted to carry mail, running daily services for about sixty years until replaced by steam railways.

The village phaeton

A light, four-wheeled carriage of the 1890s, driven from the interior, the village phaeton was designed to carry six passengers, two of whom (frequently children) faced the driver. The rear part had dos-à-dos seating in the style of a dogcart. A useful underboot was handy for small items of luggage. Drawn by a single horse or large pony, it was mounted on full elliptical springs, front and rear.

The float

The float evolved from a four-wheeled goods vehicle into a combined goods and passenger vehicle on two wheels, with a cranked axle. It was ideal for easy entry and low-loading. A popular version used by farmers for marketing was also adapted by dairymen for milk deliveries. It was usually entered through a rear door via a low step iron, although a few vehicles of this type were entered through the front. Crosswise seating was set well back in the bodywork, but many were driven from a standing

Village phaeton.

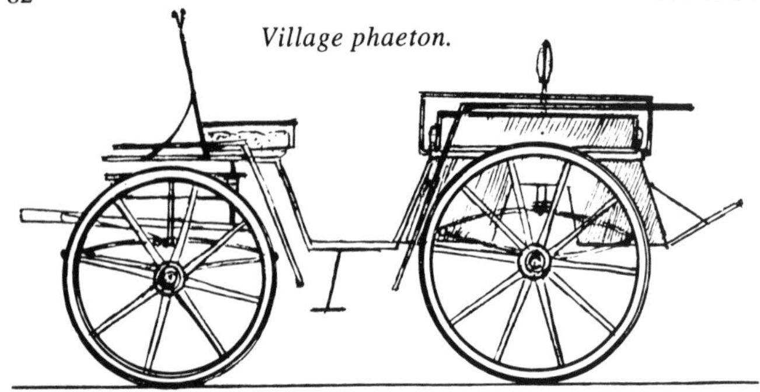

position, so allowing a better view ahead. Most had prominent splashers or mudguards. They were hung on semi-elliptical side springs and constructed in horse, cob and pony sizes, with several regional variations.

Float.

The governess car

This was in widespread use from the 1890s, although a similar type of vehicle may have been introduced, in small numbers, at least thirty years earlier. The governess car was specially designed for children in the care of a nursery governess or willing aunt. Hung fairly low on a cranked axle, it was entered through a rear door by means of a single step iron. Its use was usually confined to country lanes, private or estate roads and by-roads. It is now considered to be one of the safest owner-driven vehicles, as it is almost impossible to overturn. The main snag was its awkward, sideways-on driving position, forming part of the longitudinal seating. Suspension was in the form of semi-elliptical springs, bearing beneath a ledge-type overhang of the sides. Most governess cars had their bodywork grained and varnished rather than painted. It was usually driven to a small pony or donkey. A slightly larger but less elegant version was known as the 'tub cart'.

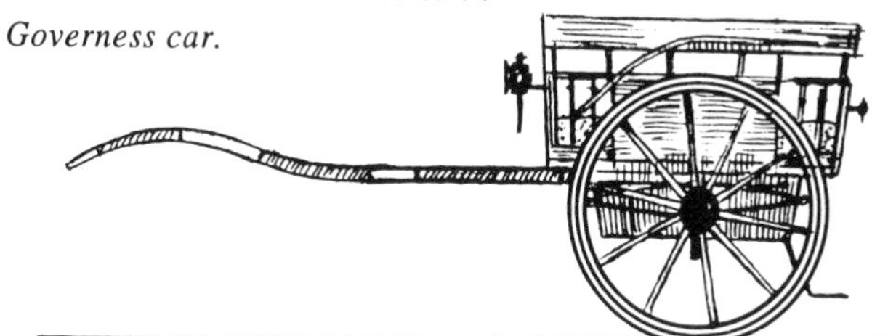

Governess car.

The wagonette

The first vehicle of this type was introduced in about 1842, constructed by the firm of Amershams to designs by Lord Curzon. In 1845 Hoopers of London built a similar vehicle, ordered by Queen Victoria to specifications of the Prince Consort. The original version was used either by a number of passengers and their hand luggage or, with seats removed, for luggage only. This made it a useful compromise between an open carriage and a luggage van and it was widely used by families for picnic parties and outings. Seats on both sides of the interior faced inwards. The driver had an elevated seat, with straight back rest and angled footboard. It was driven either to a single horse in shafts or, less frequently, to a pair in pole gear. A later and larger version known as the

A tub cart.

A wagonette photographed in 1968 in Sark, Channel Islands.

This wagonette phaeton is a compromise between the two types of vehicle.

'Lonsdale wagonette' could be driven to a four-in-hand team. The wagonette was mounted on either elliptical or semi-elliptical leaf springs.

The brougham-wagonette

A closed or headed version of the wagonette, introduced in about 1887, the brougham-wagonette usually had a bow-shaped fore-end. The seating allowed six per side with room for two or three sharing a box seat. A convertible, it could be driven open in fine weather. It would cost about 90 guineas, making it one of the cheapest four-wheeled passenger vehicles on the market. A brougham, seating only two passengers, would have cost at least 140 guineas.

The charabanc

Introduced during the 1840s as a French sporting vehicle, popular at race meetings and for shooting and hunting parties, the charabanc could be driven either to a four-in-hand team or to a pair in pole gear. There would be two or more rows of crosswise seating, the driver's seat and the first row of passenger seats being dos-à-dos. There was also a separate rear seat, at a slightly lower level, for the groom. Most had a slatted underboot, above the forecarriage, similar to the dogcart phaeton.

While the charabanc was first used almost exclusively by wealthy upper-class establishments, it was later enlarged, with extra seating, for school or works outings and tourist sightseeing, becoming a cheaper version of the tourist coach. The so-called 'roof-seat brake' was a similar type of vehicle. Charabancs were mounted on semi-elliptical leaf springs.

Charabanc.

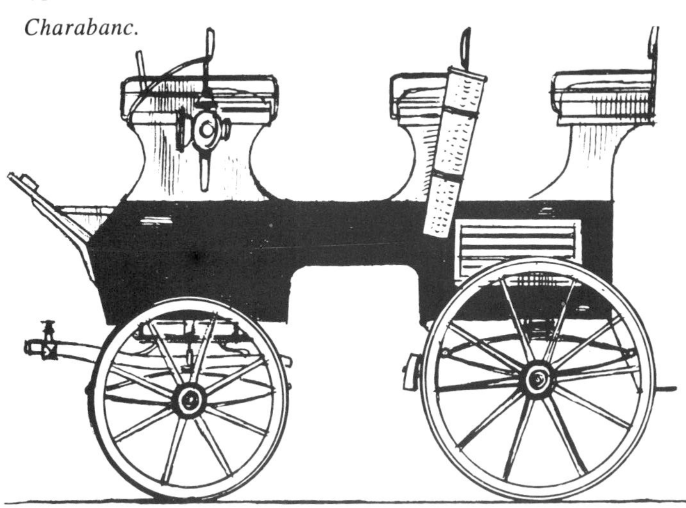

The first charabanc to appear in Britain was presented to Queen Victoria by Louis Philippe, King of the French. It is still preserved in the Royal Mews, Buckingham Palace.

Brakes (breaks)

These somewhat ungainly versions of the wagonette were introduced during the late 1860s. They were vehicles of general utility, driven either by their owner or more usually by a professional coachman. Frequently used for training and exercise purposes, they were driven either to a pair or a four-in-hand team. In the days when people of rank and wealth owned several different houses and hunting or shooting lodges (boxes) in different parts of the country, brakes would be used for taking luggage and small items of furniture from place to place. In the latter case the brake might be described as a cross between a phaeton and a fourgon, on a larger scale than either. The brake was mounted on semi-elliptical leaf springs, front and rear. Several are still in use at the Royal Mews, helping to train coach and carriage horses for ceremonial duties and the rigours of London traffic.

The body brake

An even larger vehicle than the standard brake, the body brake was frequently adapted for sightseeing trips and public outings, or even for military use, transporting large numbers of infantry in the days before mechanisation and motorisation. As with the standard brake and wagonette, it had longitudinal seating on either side of the bodywork,

Body brake.

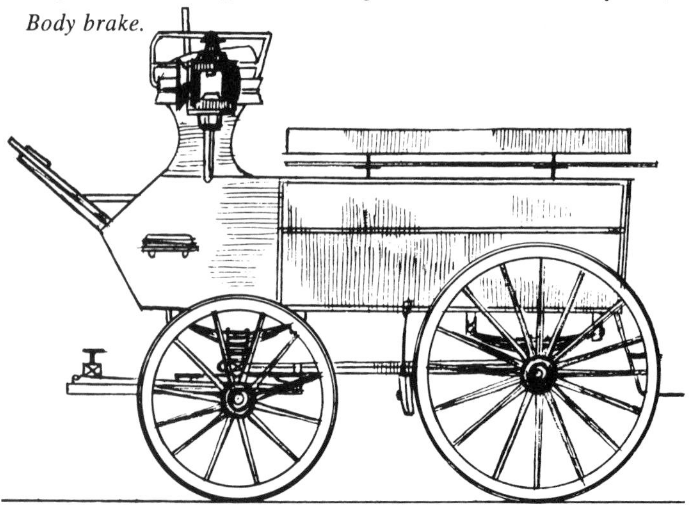

This two-horse body brake of 1895 was in use until the 1920s.

facing inwards. It was entered through a rear door by means of folding steps. A version known as the 'shooting brake' had a slatted underboot for gun dogs.

The skeleton brake

This was used by professional horse dealers and breakers to school horses for harness work, on an elementary rather than an advanced level. It was little more than an open framework with a high box seat and a small rearward platform for a groom. It was driven to a pair of horses in pole gear, one of which would be more experienced, serving as much as the driver to instruct and steady its younger partner. At the first signs of trouble, however, the groom jumped down and took the horses' heads. Some horse breakers, including those employed by main-line railway companies, which needed large numbers of horses for delivery vehicles, used a two-wheeled version or 'breaking cart'.

7
Commercial, utility, military and agricultural vehicles

TRADE VEHICLES

The forerunners of most commercial and trade vehicles were ox-drawn wagons made of roughly hewn timber. During the medieval period, at least in the western world, they were employed mainly to convey raw materials and produce to market centres or places of storage and distribution. As civilisation became more complex, special vehicles, drawn either by oxen or by heavy horses, were developed for carting timber, building materials, food and fuel. Specialised low-slung drays or trucks gradually evolved to handle bales, casks and other containers, adapted either to shafts or pole gear. Their numbers greatly increased and their types became more varied from the start of the industrial revolution, in the second half of the eighteenth century. Many new types emerged in the Victorian era as a result of changing social structures, with greater emphasis being placed on commercial needs through retail distribution; this process continued into the twentieth century. Some later types have been preserved to the present day, either for reasons of crude economy or sentiment, while others play a useful part in film and television productions, as well as in promotional and publicity enterprises. Some have been restored, through the interest of enthusiasts, but it is unfortunate that far fewer commercial vehicles have been displayed in museums than examples of passenger carriages.

Later general-purpose types

General-purpose vehicles of the mid nineteenth century remained in daily use for at least eighty years; they were frequently four-wheeled wagons, with either square or bow fronts, able to carry between 4 and 6 tons and costing from £45 to £60. These were strongly made but comparatively light, with outer raves or side boards to support an overhanging load. They were considered ideal for brewers and could be fitted with hoops or tilts for weather-proof covers. The driver usually sat fairly high, above the forecarriage. They were mostly sprung vehicles mounted on semi-elliptical leaf springs, drawn by a single horse, pairs or a larger team, according to load. A good medium-heavy horse could draw up to 2 tons.

Lighter deliveries would be made by tradesmen with much smaller vehicles, frequently known as vans, also fully sprung, and costing between £20 and £35. These could be used, like larger general-purpose vehicles, either open or covered (headed), driven to lighter horses or cobs. The ideal horse, in size between a cob and a small carthorse, was known as a 'vanner' or 'half-legged' horse and would have the minimum

A typical medium-heavy van: 1 elliptical springs, 2 shafts, 3 footboard, 4 canopy, 5 tailboard, 6 scroll iron, 7 semi-elliptical springs, 8 futchels, 9 head or cover, 10 lamp bracket.

amount of fetlock or 'feather' normally associated with much larger draught horses. Vehicles provided with hand-lever or pedal brakes were slightly more expensive, but much safer than ordinary types. In some trades two-wheeled vans or carts were found to be cheaper to maintain than heavier four-wheelers.

At first, few vehicles of any type were fitted with brakes, although these became universal before the end of the nineteenth century. Some

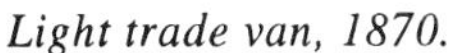
Light trade van, 1870.

A heavy delivery wagon, as used by haulage contractors from the 1860s.

larger wagons had screw-down brakes only, but also relied on the use of drag shoes when descending steep gradients. Heavier wagons made full use of a supporting underperch, while the extent of underlock was strictly limited by the size of the forewheels. The turning circle was greatly improved in later years, especially with factory-built vehicles, through the introduction of smaller forewheels and a fifth wheel or turntable of circular metal plates. This formed part of the undercarriage, held in place by a through or king pin.

The heavy or commercial float

This was of much sturdier construction than the passenger, farmer's or dairyman's float of the 1890s. It first appeared during the mid nineteenth century, mounted on a cranked axle for low-loading purposes. Unlike other floats, it rarely had mudguards or splashers. Some of the early floats or 'floaters' were extended to four wheels, especially those used to convey prize cattle, while some were used as horse ambulances. The two-wheeled type may have descended from a much earlier 'stone cart', but frequently it had higher sides and outraves to protect both wheels and overhanging loads. The traditional stone cart, however, would be much higher at the front, almost in the style of a Roman chariot. There were three main types of commercial float, all mounted on cranked axles, with semi-elliptical springs, large wheels and ramp-like tailboards. The lighter or cob-sized vehicle was ideal for street

Brewer's float.

deliveries and had a capacity of up to 15 cwt (762 kg). The medium draught-horse type carried 20 cwt (1016 kg), while the heavy draught version coped with $1^{1}/_{2}$ tons (1524 kg). Each of these cost between £30 and £35.

Vehicles for brewers and vintners

Brewers, especially, and vintners, or wine merchants, have been among the most loyal supporters of horse transport, from the later seventeenth century to the present day. The firm of Whitbreads, based in the City of London and founded during the mid eighteenth century, owns an interesting replica of a two-horse, two-wheeled dray, of a type popular from the 1700s to the 1890s. It may be said to represent a prototype not only of vehicles for delivering beer in casks and barrels, but of early drays and delivery vehicles in general. Barrels would have been carried in a crosswise position, with the drayman, in control of a tandem pair, sitting on the first barrel. The lead horse would be guided by a trouncer or drayman's mate walking beside the team.

Two-wheeled brewer's dray, eighteenth century.

There were numerous different types of dray, van, float and trolley used by brewers throughout the nineteenth century. Some are still in use, if only for publicity purposes, although it has been claimed that for deliveries within a small radius horses are cheaper than motor lorries. On early drays, both two- and four-wheeled, barrels would be placed in a sideways-on position, frequently tilted towards the centre, in double rows. Most drays or delivery wagons (some later versions similar to a so-called 'market wagon') would be drawn either by a single horse or a pair in pole gear. Much depended on distance and capacity, but a pair of horses was considered more economical and better value for average

A brewer's dray from Daniel Thwaite's brewery in Blackburn, Lancashire.

A brewer's dray delivering bottled beer in crates in Sandwich, Kent, c.1900.

needs. Some brewers and vintners used a medium-sized two-wheeled delivery float for both barrels and crates, but these were less familiar than four-wheelers.

The more recent type of brewer's dray or wagon had either high or low sides, the typical dray having upright stanchions and protective side chains. Barrels would be loaded from a platform or bay on the same level as the vehicle platform and unloaded by means of a pair of skids carried below the tail of the vehicle. The driver's seat would be fairly high above the forecarriage, attached to front boards by vertical irons or brackets and with an angled footboard. It was often a double seat large enough to share with the trouncer, although he sometimes stood on the forepart of the loading platform to one side of the driving position.

While a single-horse type carried six barrels, a dray drawn by a pair loaded between ten and twelve barrels. There were both open and covered vehicles; hoops or tilts to support a canvas top could be removed from their side sockets when not in use. There were several regional types, among the more outstanding being the 'London dray' and the 'South Wales dray', both strongly reinforced with iron stays. The London type was remarkable for its book box for paperwork, forming part of the driver's seat. Elliptical and semi-elliptical leaf springs, in different combinations, were used throughout both the nineteenth and twentieth centuries. Later vehicles usually had a shorter wheelbase but were higher above road level, with better underlock. Hand-lever, pedal and screw-down brakes were all used from the mid nineteenth century.

Vehicles of coal merchants

Coal merchants, like brewers, were among the first tradesmen to make extensive use of horse-drawn vehicles. An obvious prototype in this sphere was the London coal trolley or wagon, frequently misnamed a 'coal cart'. It first appeared during the second half of the eighteenth century, then known as Moore's patent coal carriage (named after its designer and patentee). A similar wagon was still widely used until the late 1950s. It was a spindle-sided (with vertical, open spindles), bow-fronted vehicle, with a low but solid tailboard that could be let down on chains. There would be a tray-like structure for scales and weights under the rear part of the loading platform. The large, well-dished wheels were usually painted bright red, with polished brass nuts securing the hubs. Early types would be dead-axle, although semi-elliptical leaf springs appeared from the mid Victorian era. Some had a box-like driving seat or narrow bench behind the foremost spindles at the bowed end, although others were driven from a standing position. A deep nameboard, at the bowed end, was also a prominent feature. These vehicles were mainly confined to the London area and Home Counties.

Spindle-sided trolleys or wagons were rivalled, if not ousted, by less attractive open drays that could also have an upright front or name board

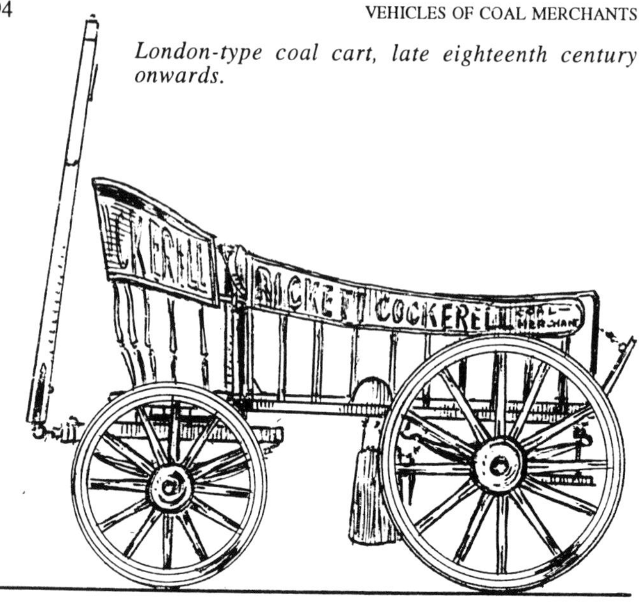

London-type coal cart, late eighteenth century onwards.

fixed to a row of vertical iron rods. Some had a midline or longitudinal structure of iron rails, dividing the loading platform into halves. Upright sacks of bagged coal lined this partition on each side. Prices would be chalked up on a semicircular wooden board, attached to either the platform or the partition. This type of vehicle, although seen in most parts of London, was even more popular in the provinces, where the

South of England coal cart.

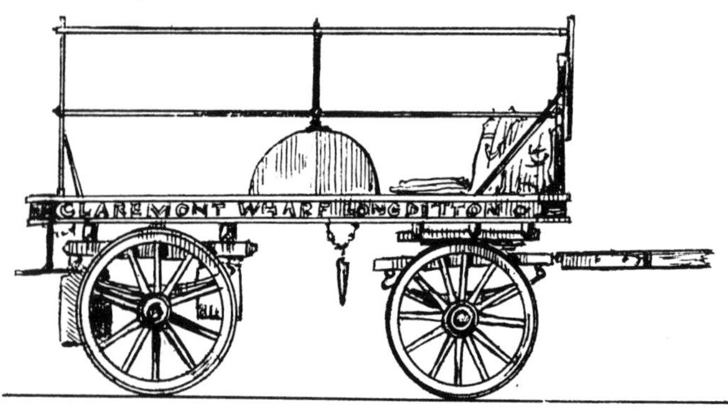

A London coal cart.

descendants of Moore's coal carriage were rarely seen. The majority were led through the streets when loaded, but driven back to the wharf or coal yard with the driver standing braced against the front board. Brakes were seldom used, apart from the odd screw-down type, although all coal trolleys carried a drag shoe.

Vehicles used by builders and contractors

Builders made frequent use of horse-drawn vehicles until the 1940s, especially two-wheeled tip carts; similar types were also used in brick-works and quarries. They were available in large, medium and small horse sizes, for Shire types, medium draught horses and cobs. Factory-built versions were turned out in large numbers and advertised in trade journals such as *The Clay Worker* until shortly after the Second World War.

The traditional builder's cart, with adequate side boards or raves to protect the wheels from an overhanging load, also had flat but forward-inclined front boards. It would hold about six hundred bricks and cost between £16 and £26 when new. This would be for a medium-weight draught horse. The London builder's cart, of even sturdier construction, was panel-sided, with its front boards projecting even further forward, and it had detachable side boards of greater width than on provincial types. Shafts would be supported by propsticks when the cart rested; a prop was slung beneath each shaft and lowered from horizontal to vertical.

Dressed stone or marble was frequently brought to building sites on

A London builder's cart.

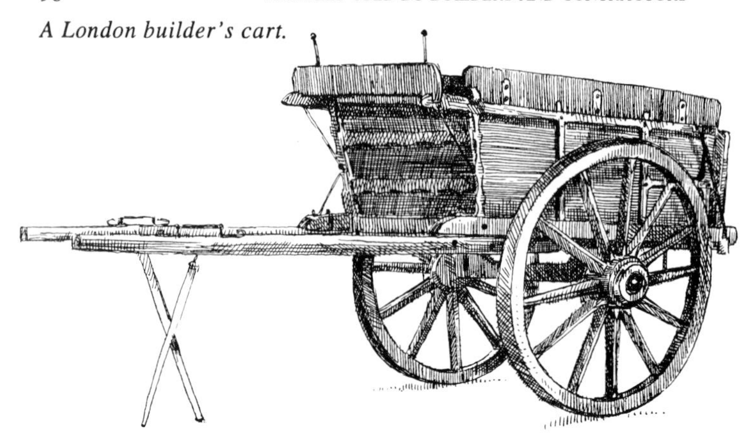

low-sided carts, with high-bowed front boards and large wheels on cranked axles. These would be drawn by a single heavy horse in straight shafts, although sometimes assisted by a second or chain horse in tandem.

Towards the end of the nineteenth century there were also a number of four-wheeled trolleys or wagons for builders, drawn by either a single horse in shafts or a pair in pole gear. These were plank- or panel-sided, driven from a single cross-seat raised on irons or brackets above the forecarriage. They cost between £45 and £65, according to size and finish. Although frequently termed vans, they were seldom headed but may have had tarpaulin covers drawn over the hoops or tilts. Screw-down brakes were evident, but drag shoes were used more frequently.

Stone or marble cart.

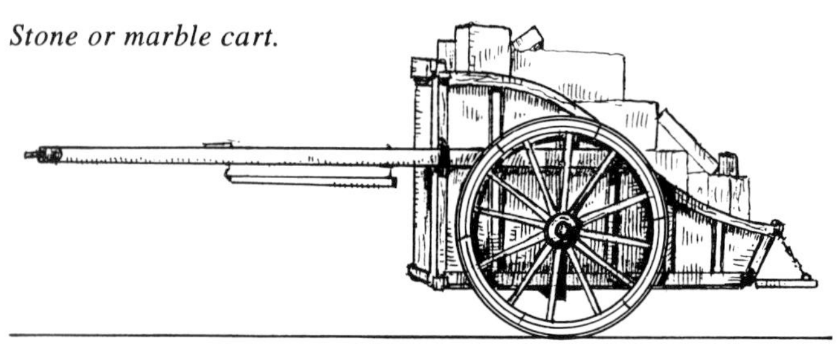

Bakery vehicles

Retail bakers mainly used hand carts for delivery work until the mid nineteenth century, after which more prosperous tradesmen preferred either two- or four-wheeled horse-drawn delivery vans. The first type of bread van was a gig-like vehicle having a square or oblong compartment

Bread van.

for the merchandise, which was loaded through a rear door. A single driving seat with side irons and an angled footboard would be fitted at the front of the compartment above its slightly arched top. A side rail enclosed upper space, in which spare baskets might be lodged. A low-slung but more upright and fully enclosed vehicle, with an inner cross-seat, was known as a 'coburg'. This had a cranked axle, its body mounted on semi-elliptical leaf springs – as were the earlier gig types.

A Birmingham Co-operative Society Bakery Department van, 1961.

An early twentieth-century bread van, now in the collection of the Leicestershire Museums, Arts and Records Service.

A 1930s bread van on pneumatic tyres. It was built at the Co-operative Wholesale Society works in Manchester.

London Co-operative Society bakery van in Ilford in 1949.

Four-wheeled vans appeared towards the end of the Victorian era, but they frequently competed with both coburgs and higher but straight-axled two-wheelers. From the late 1930s many were replaced by motor vans or electric trucks. Both two- and four-wheelers would be drawn by a 'vanner', cob or large pony. They were either ledge vans, with a certain amount of overhang above their waistline, or straight-sided. Roofs would be either rounded or of crosswise 'D' section, but less frequently straight and flat-topped, inclining slightly downward above the driving position. The fore-end was usually protected by a dashboard of medium height. The angled floorboard was rare on this type. Some vans had small windows or lights on either side of the driving position. Suspension of four-wheelers would be by full elliptical springs at the front and semi-ellipticals at the rear. Both pedal and screw-down brakes were acceptable, but especially the latter. Common or drabble axles were frequently used, although more expensive types, with better finish, had mail-coach hubs and axles. During the period between the world wars some bakery vans, along with other trade vehicles, acquired disc wheels with pneumatic tyres. These vehicles were usually equirotal, the wheels fitting under the vehicle and sometimes having motor-car type mudguards. Modern types also had sliding side panels for access to the rear compartment, in place of the rear doors.

Butchery vehicles

High-class butchers prided themselves on a swift efficient delivery service, which frequently ran twice a day. Their delivery boys, wearing striped aprons and straw hats, drove fully enclosed pony-sized vehicles of the gig type, often at a dangerous pace. A smart turnout with a quality animal between the shafts turned most heads and proved an excellent

London butcher's cart.

advertisement. Like early bread carts, the single driving seat would be top-front, with an angled footboard reached via shaft steps. Shafts curved slightly upwards towards the extremities and the bodywork tilted in a rearward direction. A single iron or brass rail enclosed the top or head. Similar vehicles were also used by better-class fishmongers and for the collection of newspapers at main-line railway stations. All types were well ventilated with side slats or perforations and lined with zinc for improved insulation. They were mounted on semi-elliptical leaf

A typical butcher's cart c.1900.

The first design of mobile butcher's shop, built in 1923 by the Co-operative Wholesale Society.

springs. A four-wheeled butcher's van that resembled a dogcart phaeton was used in some areas, but it was not widely popular.

During the late 1920s and early 1930s there were a number of vehicles owned by the Co-operative Society and a few large departmental stores, servicing new housing estates and outlying suburbs. These were fully enclosed and might be described as mobile shops. They had large display windows, built-in refrigerators and serving hatches, with racks on which large joints of meat or quarters could be hung. Drawn by a single horse in shafts, they were equirotal on pneumatic tyres. They were usually driven from the interior, although the prototype of 1923 had an exterior box seat at the fore-end. The prototype also had iron-shod wheels.

Fishmongers' vehicles

Apart from the enclosed or box type of vehicle previously mentioned, fishmongers delivered or hawked from house to house with open, low-sided carts. These would be pony-sized, having slatted side panels or planks, and were mounted on semi-elliptical springs. There would also be a high, fixed tailboard. Much larger and higher carts were to be found in coastal areas and fishing villages, not only selling fish but driving into shallow water to meet incoming boats in places where it might be difficult to approach the quay. Some carts, although more like the conventional farm cart or tumbril, were even used in trawling for

Fishmonger's cart.

shrimps and other shellfish, especially on the Lancashire coast, as horses know by instinct where to avoid quicksands, wading well above their hocks. Such carts, of which there is an example in Merseyside Maritime Museum, were even fitted out with lamps and compasses, useful in times of fog or sea-mist.

Milk delivery vehicles

For many years milk deliveries were made with three-wheeled hand carts, types appearing in the West End of London well into the 1930s. The low-slung dairy float on cranked axles, although seemingly traditional, was not widely used until the 1890s. This proved ideal for the large milk churns of the day, some mounted on gimbals to prevent jolting and souring the milk. As they were low-loaders and near to ground level

A fish merchant's cart unloading on the foreshore at Scarborough, North Yorkshire, c.1910.

Manchester milk float.

it was much easier to manhandle churns in and out of the vehicle than to lift them on to a higher loading platform. Some dairymen, however, preferred a four-wheeled, open vehicle, although with slatted sides, raised to a certain level. In less exclusive areas milk might be served into jugs or bowls, at street level, churns having a stop-tap that projected in a rearward direction through apertures of the tailboard. Such vehicles would be mounted on elliptical springs and driven from a cross-seat above the forecarriage. In better-class districts milk would be taken to the tradesmen's entrance, in covered pails, and ladled into household vessels over the threshold.

In later years, when bottled milk replaced churns and pails, floats were less frequently used, superseded by four-wheeled milk wagons, some

Milk delivery box van.

Light sprung milk cart.

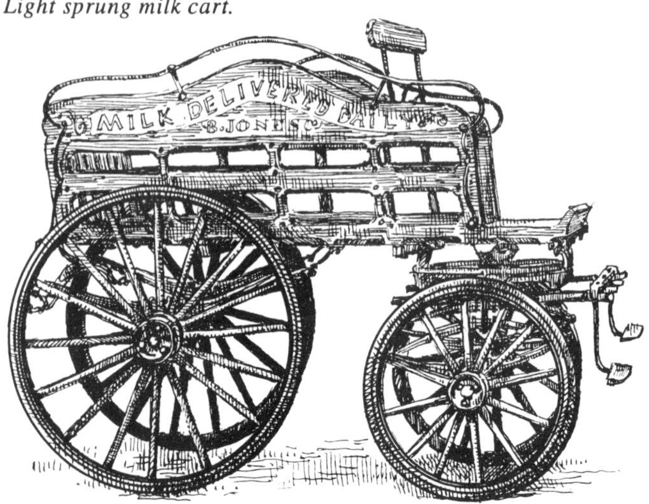

eventually running on pneumatic tyres. Milk delivery vehicles of all types were among the first to use rubber rather than iron tyres, to help deaden the noise of early morning deliveries in residential suburbs. The milk wagon, often known as a 'box cart', had a single driving seat at the front, on an extension of the loading platform above the fore-axle. Many

A London dairyman's float with two churns, 1901.

A milk delivery van from the north of England, c.1928.

A 'step-in' milk delivery van in use with the Slough and District Co-operative Society, Berkshire, in the 1930s.

A box-type milk delivery van, belonging to Handsworth Dairies in Birmingham, 1951.

of this type had offside pedal brakes, operated from the driving position. Some also had screw-down hand brakes. Bottles in crates were conveyed within an enclosed body, access being through sliding panels on each side. Empty crates might be transferred to a roof rack. There would be full underlock or cut-under of the forewheels and semi-elliptical suspension, front and rear. During the 1900s a step-in milk wagon was introduced, of a type first used in the United States of America. These were fully enclosed, driven from the interior with reins passed through an aperture of the windscreen. Although well-protected for all-weather driving, easy to mount and load, manipulation of the reins was difficult, even dangerous, and not widely accepted by British dairies.

After the Second World War a number of odd-looking delivery vehicles were constructed for the larger dairies. Most had bodywork of light metal alloys, with small front wheels fitting close together. Although mounted on pneumatic tyres, they were so badly designed for draught purposes that they were known as 'horse killers'.

Grocery vans

Grocery vans for the delivery of dry goods and branded items in tins, jars and bottles might have been low, box-like trolleys on four wheels, headed and fully enclosed, or much higher panel-sided carts. The latter were either flat- or round-topped, frequently ledged to overhang the wheels. There would be a low footboard or toeboard in place of the angled footboard and dashboard. The driving seat would be a cross-bench spanning the entire width of the forepart. Further back in the body of the vehicle would be shelves and compartments for the wares. Many comestibles such as tea, sugar, rice and flour were measured out and

A two-wheeled grocer's delivery van at Epping, Essex, in 1902, decorated for the coronation of Edward VII.

weighed from bulk quantities in the vehicle, rather than ready-packed.

Greengrocery vehicles

Fresh vegetables, fruit and cut flowers were sold in London streets from long barrow-like carts that could be pushed manually or drawn by a single pony in shafts. There were also costermonger carts, the open framework of their sides sloping to the base of the shafts from a much higher back board. These were both two- and four-wheeled, but mainly the former, having small wheels for their overall size and lengthwise semi-elliptical springs. In all towns, many street traders, especially those with daily rounds, preferred an open or low-sided trolley or pony dray. These might have demountable covers in waterproof material, set on hoops, for all-weather trading. In the north of England flat open vehicles for street trading and collection or delivery services were known as 'Bradford carts', hauled by a sturdy pony or small cob. They were driven from a sitting or standing position at the front of the loading platform, while a number had driving seats on raised brackets or stanchions across the full width at the fore-end.

Various branches of the Co-operative Society showed great initiative

A hawker's cart used for greengrocery in Forest Gate, London, in 1949.

in this sphere during the 1920s and 1930s, using a wide range of headed vehicles, mainly on four wheels, for door-to-door sales of fruit and vegetables. Most of these would be open on both sides, with items displayed in neat trays, some having storage lockers below the loading platform or at roof level. Both ends of such vehicles would be boarded up or fitted with solid panels. Shutters or roller-blinds protected the interior in harsh weather. The driver's seat, on an extension of the fore-

A large van on pneumatic tyres, used to supply hotels and restaurants with greengroceries.

end, might be partly enclosed under a canopy or in a half-cab, with a cross-bench and sidelights. Suspension would be on semi-elliptical springs, while the wheels had pneumatic tyres, with or without mudguards.

An even earlier trolley, appearing mainly in the Greater London area up to and less often after the Second World War, was known as the 'hawker's cart' and ran on four wheels with semi-elliptical springs. These were mainly used for fruit and vegetables but could be adapted to handle anything from firewood to hardware and strings of onions. The lower part or platform was similar to the totter's dray or trolley, although frequently headed with a hood or canopy drawn over tilts. A modern version, loaded with selected fruits, now frequently appears in trade classes at horse shows in the Home Counties, but these usually have a shorter wheelbase and pneumatic tyres. Screw-down brakes are a feature of most types.

Totter's trolleys

Also known as a 'totter's cart' or 'dray', this type of flat open vehicle was used by scrap-metal merchants and general dealers for street collections, especially in the London area. It was similar to the hawker's cart but with a shorter wheelbase than the more traditional type. A driving seat, raised on curved and vertical irons or brackets, would be mounted at the fore-end and reached by shaft steps. The original version had small forewheels with iron tyres for cut-under and improved lock, but these were later replaced by equirotals on pneumatic tyres. Totters' trolleys were mounted on semi-elliptical springs. The shafts were either straight or slightly curved at the extremities.

Tankers

These were seen in both town and country, mainly from the late 1890s to the early 1920s, and used for any type of bulk liquid from water to fuel oil and paraffin. Large numbers were used from the 1900s by the emerging petrol companies, when motor cars were still a rich man's hobby and before motorised tankers were introduced.

Most tankers would be driven to a pair of medium-heavy draught horses in pole gear, although single horses and larger teams were not unknown. They would be controlled from a cab-like semi-enclosed box seat with angled footboard. A few, however, especially smaller types driven to a single horse, had open seats. The general structure consisted of a cylindrical tank in horizontal form, with top fillers, mounted between crosswise and lengthwise members of a wooden still. There would be much smaller wheels at the front, which were able to turn in full lock. A shelf-like tray for small cans would be fitted down each side of the tank. Mounted on semi-elliptical springs, this vehicle had lever, pedal or screw-down brakes.

Tanker.

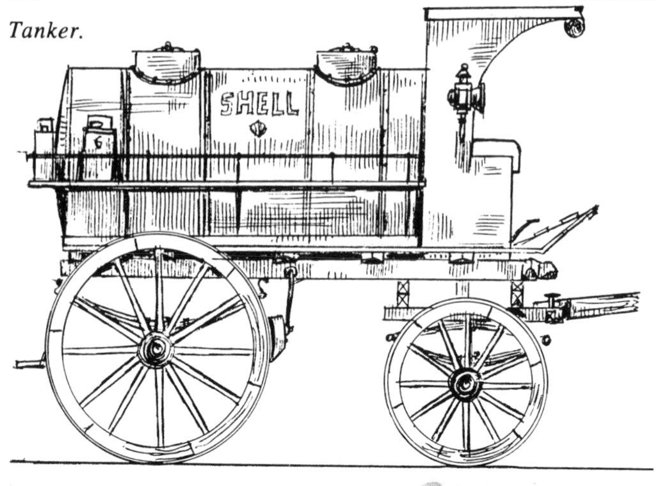

An oil tanker in the 1900s.

Laundry vans

There were two main types of laundry van, one slightly larger than the other. Both were four-wheeled, mounted on elliptical or semi-elliptical springs. The more popular version, widely seen throughout the provinces, outwardly resembled a large baker's or bread van. It had rear doors and would be stacked inside with wickerwork laundry baskets. Some vans, however, had access through the front only, while others had tailboards, letting down through 90 degrees, with two flap or half-doors above. Most were straight-sided.

An earlier and perhaps more traditional van (although some survived until the 1940s, mainly in the London area) had a high square body with

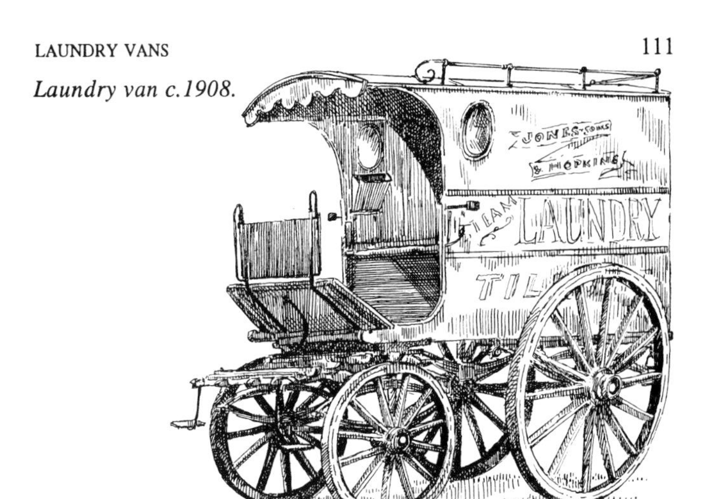

Laundry van c.1908.

planked rather than panelled sides. This might be headed with a canvas top stretched over tilts. There would be a driver's seat or cross-bench spanning the entire width, with a low footboard and extended canopy.

Vehicles of tailors, hatters and haberdashers

Fashionable tailors, hatters and haberdashers frequently ran delivery services for their favoured customers. For this they used light, four-wheeled vehicles, sometimes 'hybrids' developed from a combination

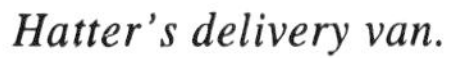

Hatter's delivery van.

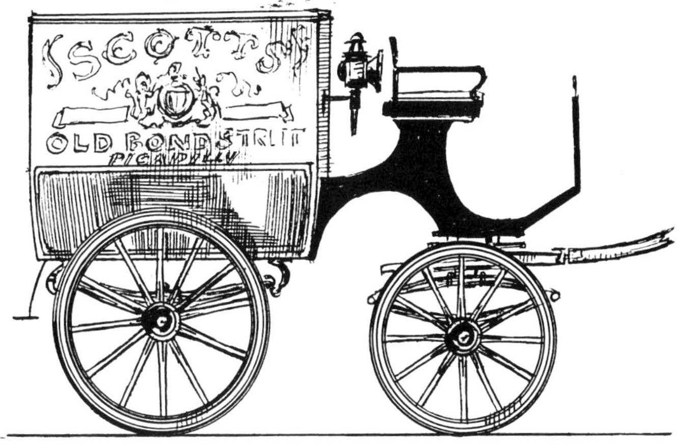

Draper's coburg.

of two different types rather than custom-built. Considerable use was made of the brougham or omnibus van: for example, a square, fully enclosed body, with rear doors and a box seat, mounted on elliptical springs, could have had the underworks of a brougham. Many hybrids had a van body above the lower structure of a wagonette. Drawn by a single horse or pony, most had a double driving seat. Some tailors also used a two-wheeled coburg.

Omnibus van or brougham van.

An omnibus van owned by Rothmans of Pall Mall.

Furniture vans

Horse-drawn furniture vans or pantechnicons were a familiar sight from the 1870s to the 1930s. Even when no longer drawn by horses, their pole gear (for a pair or a larger team) would be exchanged for drawbars to suit mechanical haulage. Several were even coupled together as a road train. If the removal was over a considerable distance most of the journey would be made by rail: the vans would be drawn to the nearest station by horses and rolled on to a flat carriage truck from an end loading bay. They would be met at the station nearest their destination by a hired team ordered in advance.

Both large and small vans would be constructed on the same lines, having long low-slung bodies with a deep well forming the rear half of their construction. The large rear wheels, on cranked axles, fitted in recesses that arched above them, the much smaller front wheels turning in full lock. At the rear an ample tailboard could be let down to form a loading ramp. The driver's seat, with side irons and angled footboard, would be at or near roof level, while the flat or slightly curved roof (of crosswise D-shaped section) would have deep rounding boards. These helped to form an upper compartment for certain items of furniture, standard lamps and rolls of carpet or linoleum. They also provided a flat surface that could be used for advertising. Suspension would be in the form of semi-elliptical springs front and rear.

Furniture van, 1901.

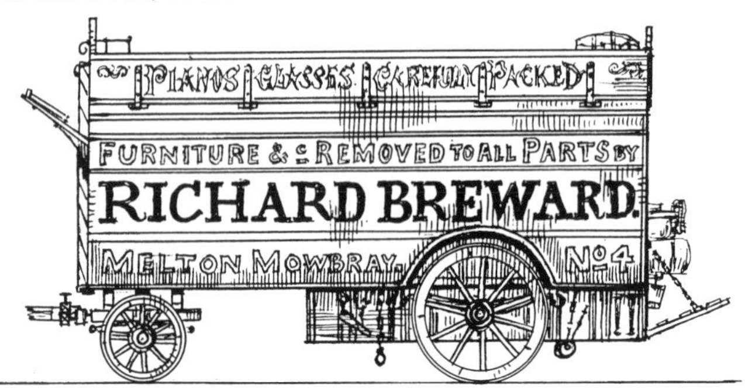

Some furniture vans had small equirotal wheels, but these were exceptional. From the 1900s a lift-off container body was introduced so that loads could be transferred from the dray-like undergear either to a railway truck or to the hold of a ship, especially if for transhipment overseas. For extra strength, the side planking of furniture vans was frequently diagonal, set towards a centre point on the vertical plane to give a chevron effect.

Ice and icecream vehicles

Ice carts or vans (usually four-wheelers) were to be seen in large cities and dockland areas until the First World War and the development of more sophisticated systems of refrigeration. The London version (a similar type also appearing in provincial centres) would be headed, panel-sided and fully enclosed, having the driving seat partly sheltered

A furniture pantechnicon, built in 1896 for Abels of St Albans.

as a half-cab and being drawn either by a single horse or by a pair in pole gear. The lettering on the sides would be in a florid, colourful style, usually the name of some Italian firm or proprietor as that nationality had a monopoly in this line of business. Large quantities of ice came to London and east-coast ports, either in Norwegian ships or from the Baltic, and were transferred in blocks to fully insulated road vehicles at the quayside.

Icecream carts were also the near monopoly of Italian firms or individuals. Although some ran on four wheels and were not true carts, the majority were two-wheeled and merely an enlarged version of the hand barrow. Some, like the costermonger's fruit barrow, could be adapted for either pony or manual draught. Both cranked and straight axles were used, but the former were preferred. A protective canopy and striped awning, with deep valances, were supported by diagonal brass standards in barley-sugar twists that smacked of fairground locations, where many such vehicles might be found. Highly polished metalwork and colourful lettering were essential features of decor.

Railway cartage vehicles

Most railway-owned vehicles, apart from a few reserved for internal or maintenance work at large depots, belonged to the cartage department. They were as varied as the consignments of merchandise sent by rail and included open wagons, light and heavy parcel vans, drays, timber carriages and low-loading trolleys for boilers and heavy machinery.

Most of these were used by the main-line companies until nationalisation and shortly afterwards, a declining number being retained by British Railways until the mid 1950s. As late as 1928 there were 32,171 carts, vans and drays in daily use with only 2837 motor vehicles. These figures do not include independent, joint and subsidiary companies such as the Metropolitan Railway and Great Northern Joint Committee lines, all of which had a large number of horse-drawn delivery vans.

Perhaps the most popular and widely used vehicle was the single-horse wagon, although sometimes driven to a pair. This type would pull up to a capacity of 2 tons, the recognised limit in the London area being 1¾ tons for a single horse and 3½ tons for a pair. The single-horse wagon had full underlock of the forecarriage and was mounted on semi-elliptical springs front and rear. There would be a driving seat raised on vertical irons or brackets above the headboards, with an angled footboard. Lever or pedal brakes acted on the rear wheels, while all vehicles carried a drag shoe. Slatted sides would be strongly reinforced with iron or steel strapwork. Hoops or tilts fitted into sockets over which a canvas or tarpaulin cover could be drawn. There was also a small but comprehensive range of much heavier wagons of this type, drawn by quality Shire horses known as 'wagoners', the pride of their stables.

An open wagon, built at Swindon in 1905, and used by the Great Western Railway for general cartage purposes.

Most companies owned a wide selection of lighter single-horse vans, attached to the luggage and parcels delivery services. The arched roofs of these would be boarded up on the inside, covered by a layer of proofed canvas or tarpaulin on the outside. Demountable sections extended downwards on either side of the lower body in a ledge effect. The average light parcels van would be 14 3/4 cwt (750 kg). Some had small

Railway parcels van, 1890.

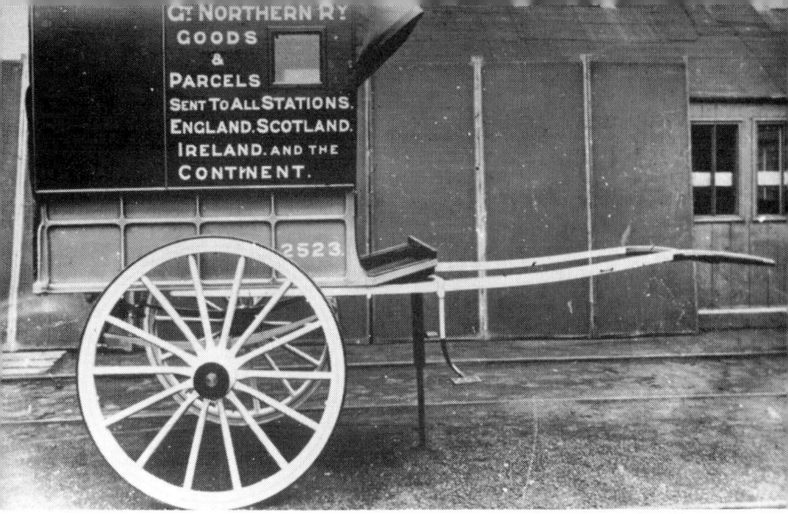

A two-wheeled parcels delivery van just completed for the Great Northern Railway at its Doncaster works c.1912.

windows on either side of the crosswise driving seat, which was well back under a canopy extension. The tailboard was let down on chains at an angle of 90 degrees. A 'van' or 'car' boy, acting as assistant, accompanied each driver, riding at the back of the van and clinging to a knotted rope. There were also two-wheeled vans or covered carts in the parcels department, some as elegant as carriages, kept for express deliveries. Many horses were quality animals of the hunter type, while ponies for lighter, two-wheeled vans may have had hackney blood.

Prize cattle destined for agricultural and fatstock shows were often taken to the station in what were known as 'bull floats', either two- or four-wheeled vehicles with cranked axles and ramp-like tailboards for low loading. Similar vehicles were also used as horse ambulances by the railway companies.

In some areas, especially the manufacturing towns of central and northern England, the single-horse dray or trolley, also known as a 'lorry' or 'rulley', was a familiar sight from the 1880s to the early 1950s. This was a flat open vehicle, either sprung or dead-axle, having screw-down brakes in some versions, but usually without a driver's seat. The single horse would be led through the streets but was often driven from a standing position on the front of the loading platform. The average trolley was 17 cwt (863 kg) tare weight, with a capacity of 2 tons. Chain horses were frequently used, in tandem, to cope with maximum loads. Most later vehicles of this type were equirotal and had detachable shafts that could be interchanged with drawbars for mechanical (tractor) haulage. During the Second World War a number were constructed without leaf springs, depending for their suspension on pneumatic tyres only.

A parcels delivery van built in 1901 at Swindon by the Great Western Railway.

A number of delivery vans survived nationalisation, while drays and trolleys were evident in fair numbers until the mid 1950s. The ultimate design in this area was a single-horse van of a type first used by the Great Western Railway at Oxford station during the late 1930s. The prototype entered regular service in October 1937 and similar vans were used in all parts of Britain for at least twenty years. They had wheels of motor-

Railway delivery van c.1930.

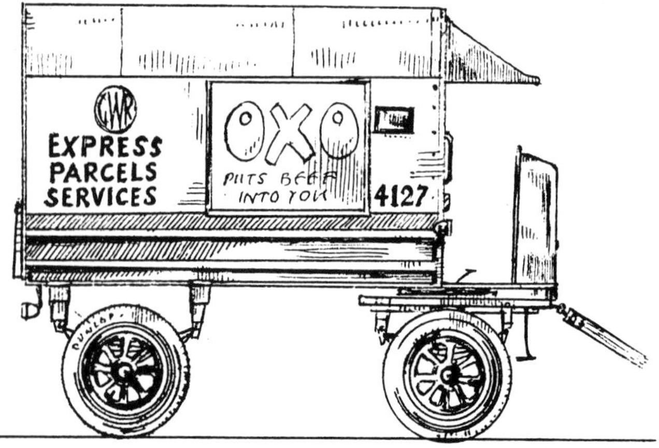

car type with pneumatic tyres, ball-bearing hubs, disc brakes and battery-powered electric headlights, among other features. A square scuttlebox dashboard resembled the radiator of a motor van, so that many laymen thought they were reconstructed from old motor vehicles.

The high-capacity low-loading vehicle previously mentioned was known as a 'boiler trolley'. A typical example was produced at the Swindon works in about 1905 and also by several other main-line companies serving industrial areas. It consisted of a low carrying frame of longitudinal steel girders, with crosswise bolsters at each end. Wheels were of the solid type, steel throughout with broad treads. Draught gear was in the form of double shafts. Its capacity was up to 40 tons and it would have been drawn by a large team of wagoners, the chain traces of the leading horses attached to the shafts of the wheelers.

A number of horse-drawn railway vehicles during the first half of the twentieth century ran on what were classed as artillery wheels. These were of a type also used on gun carriages and military supply wagons, having steel naves, dust excluders or caps and additional spokes for extra strength.

PUBLIC UTILITY AND SPECIAL VEHICLES

Almost everything portable or mounted on wheels appeared as a horse-drawn vehicle of some form, from fire engines and ambulances to various types of cart or wagon for street cleaning and refuse collection. In the days of street trams there were even 'horsed' service departments to maintain overhead wires and standards, equipped with four-wheeled ladder trucks. Roadmaking and repair departments had horse-drawn tar boilers mounted on iron wheels when the tar spraying of public highways was introduced in about 1908.

Fire engines

Primitive types of fire engine, dating back to the early eighteenth century, were hand-propelled or drawn by a single horse. They were manual-lever appliances, operated by local volunteers, serving their parish or a large country estate. Larger versions of the same vehicle were eventually drawn by a pair of horses and used by fire insurance companies, mostly in large cities and urban areas. The first engine with a steam pump was jointly invented by Braithwaite and Ericsson, both freelance engineers. It was given its first trials in 1829, mainly in the London area, and proved to be a mechanical success. However, it was first used officially by trained firefighters outside Britain, in New York and other cities. Drawn by a pair of medium or light draught horses in pole gear, it was an enlarged carrying frame for a pump and boiler, supported by iron-spoked wheels (then a novelty), also having a high-perched driving seat. Exhaust was expelled through a rearward-directed tube in the form of a coiled serpent.

Horse-drawn steam fire engines, with vertical boilers at the rear, were

Estate fire engine.

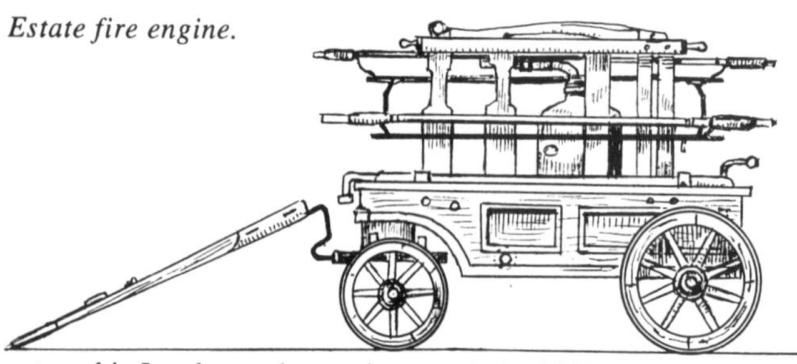

not used in London or the provinces until the 1860s, their acceptance depending on the foundation of the Metropolitan Fire Service in 1865. A typical example of this early type was the 'London vertical', an engine perfected by James Shand, widely used in all parts of Britain until the 1900s. It was also known as the '250 gallon engine', having double-acting steam cylinders able to pump that amount of water (1137 litres) per minute. The driver and officer in charge shared a box seat, while other firemen rode on longitudinal side seats facing outwards. The boiler and pump, raising steam from cold within a few minutes, would be in the care of an engineer fireman, crouched on a rear platform. There were nine men per engine, which was drawn by two or three horses, usually in pairs or three abreast, but sometimes unicorn. In the last case the third or cock horse would be ridden by a postilion. Fire-brigade horses in the London area were provided by Thomas Tilling, a contractor or job-master who was also responsible for hiring out many bus horses. Wheel horses were stabled at the station in pairs and lightweight harnesses lowered on to their bodies from above at the first note of an alarm bell. The main pump-engine would be backed up by other four-wheeled

The first horse-drawn steam fire engine.

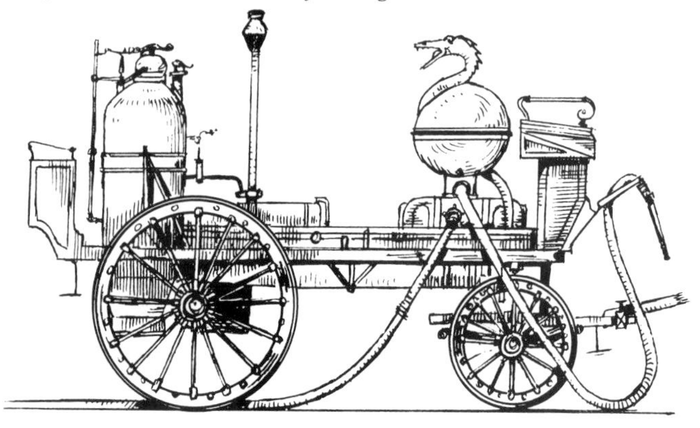

Shand-Mason fire engine c.1870.

vehicles, some manned by the volunteer salvage corps. These included an escape or extending ladder on large wheels, of a type later used by motor fire engines until the 1970s. There were also chemical engines, each provided with a large tank, which were used to quench certain types of fire or when water supplies failed.

A horse-drawn fire-engine, c.1890, in the collection of Leicestershire Museums, Arts and Records Service.

Ambulance c.1900.

Ambulances

Horse-drawn ambulances tended to be makeshift until the closing decades of the nineteenth century, although some four-wheeled cabs could be converted to take stretcher cases. The latter would be fitted with rubber tyres to cushion the patient over hard, uneven surfaces. Military ambulances were first used by the French army during the wars of the Revolutionary and Napoleonic era. They were copied by other nations and later extended to civilian duties. By the 1890s they emerged as

Horse ambulance.

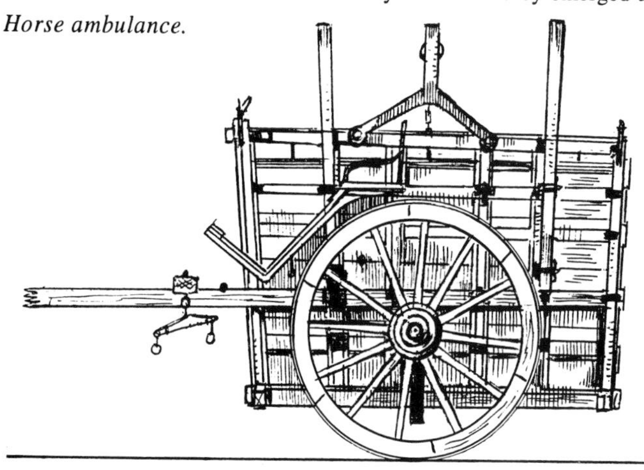

panel-sided, van-like vehicles entered from the rear via folding steps. Mounted on semi-elliptical springs, with either lever or pedal brakes, they had an open or covered box seat and pole draught for a pair of horses.

Vehicles for refuse collection and other utilities

Many local authorities used different types of horse-drawn vehicle especially to keep roads clear and dispose of refuse. Most of these were introduced during the second half of the nineteenth century, including water carts or wagons, some even fitted with revolving brushes. All types would be drawn by heavy horses of the Shire breed, always worked at a slow walking pace. Such horses and vehicles were funded by local councils, whose meetings were often held in church vestries (in the days before purpose-built council offices or chambers), and so the horses were often known as 'vestry horses'.

The covered dust cart or wagon (a cart in name only), horse-drawn until the 1930s, was eventually mounted on elliptical leaf springs and pneumatic or solid rubber tyres. Earlier types had small iron-shod wheels, usually equirotal. The top or upper part was of crosswise D-section shape, provided with sliding shutters or 'lids' over the rubbish compartments. Led rather than driven, very few had a driving seat. An open four-wheeled refuse wagon of the 1880s, widely used in the London boroughs, was the 'Margitson & Hek tip cart' (wagon), with both rearward and sideways tipping facilities, unusual for a four-wheeler. These were lined with sheet iron, having high fronts and raves or rounding boards. They were driven from a standing position on the front of the vehicle. There were three sizes, the largest advertised as having a capacity of 2½ cubic yards.

What were known as 'tumbler carts' may have been used for the disposal of damp refuse or sewage, especially in rural areas with cess pits. The inner bodies of these two-wheeled vehicles would be water-tight, rotating on a central axle. When a top lid was removed, the tank could be tipped backwards by means of rack and pinion gear on the shafts. There were three main sizes, all drawn by medium or heavy draught horses, the largest up to 200 gallons (900 litres) capacity.

The general-purpose municipal water cart was necessary for washing

Tumbler cart, late nineteenth century.

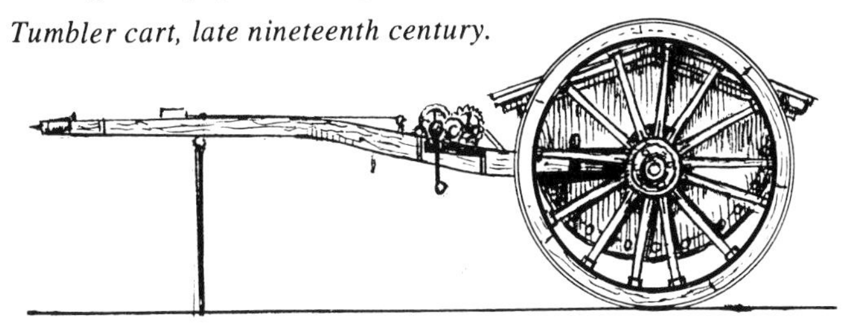

down dusty or muddy streets in urban areas. Some, of a similar type, were also used for distributing liquid manure on farmland or bringing water to outlying cottages in times of drought. The square tank of each cart or wagon (there were both two- and four-wheeled types) would be made of iron plates cemented together, fitted with both a rearward manual pump and a spreadboard or sprinkler device. Early types were dead-axle, led on foot, although later versions, especially four-wheelers, had a crosswise seat above the tank, with side irons and an angled footboard. Small-sized water tanks held up to 120 gallons (545 litres), while larger types held up to 300 gallons (1364 litres). Most were driven to a single horse in shafts.

Iron water cart, 1880.

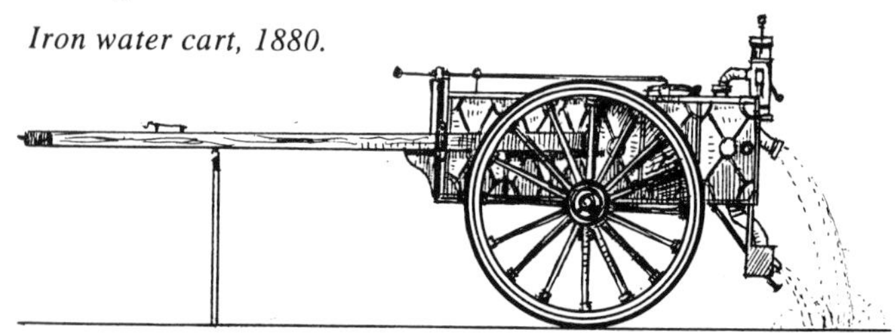

From the early 1860s many urban and municipal authorities used a four-wheeled vehicle known as a road-breaker. In the days before pneumatic drills, considerable labour with pick and shovel was saved by breaking up old road surfaces before they were relaid. The road-breaker was a panel-sided wagon, loaded with stones and scrap iron, drawn by teams of four or six horses. The front wheels were able to turn in a three-quarters lock, having iron tyres and naves. Back wheels were also iron-shod but had a double row of conical spikes set in the treads. The teams would be led rather than driven, moving at a slow walking pace, breaking up the old surfaces as they moved forward. Wheel horses were usually in double shafts.

Royal Mail vehicles

Mails were originally carried by postboys on horses, rather like the pony express of the old West. During the second half of the eighteenth century John Palmer introduced a system of nationwide mail coaches that became a byword for reliability and safety, remaining in operation for about seventy years. These were eventually replaced by railway mail vans, although in districts beyond the railhead or some distance from the nearest station there would be local services operated with horse-drawn mail carts and brougham-type vans. Some of these would also bring mail to stations and sorting offices from sub-post offices. In remote areas of the west of England there were even small donkey carts.

A much larger vehicle, developed during the 1880s, was the 'parcels

General Post Office mail van.

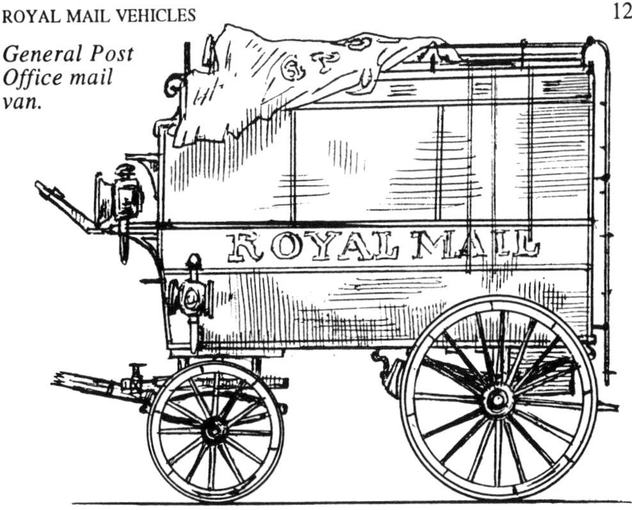

mail van', which often travelled overnight, hired by the General Post Office from the firm of McNamara & Company. This would be an enclosed box van, running on four wheels, with full lock of its forecarriage. It was suspended on elliptical springs at the front and semi-elliptical springs at the rear, and there would also be a double driving seat almost at roof level, with the angled footboard on brackets. Headlamps of mail-coach type were fixed on both sides of the vehicle. Driven to a four-in-

The London to Watford parcel mail van, 1890.

hand team, it was frequently referred to as a 'mail coach', although passengers were not carried in normal circumstances. A mail coach or van of this type ran between London and Chatham until the summer of 1908, although it is difficult to imagine why this should have supplemented or replaced an adequate railway service. There were at least half a dozen mail-van routes out of London until 1909, one reaching as far west as Oxford.

During the Second World War horse-drawn vans were revived by the Post Office, especially in London, to save petrol. These, like the older mail vans, were also the responsibility of McNamara. They were strictly for local work and resembled four-wheeled bakery vans but were painted in the scarlet livery of the GPO. Drawn by a single horse of the vanner or small cob type, most were equirotal, with pneumatic tyres. A few survived until the early 1950s.

Undertakers' vehicles

The mystique of a large-scale funeral was an essential part of Victorian social life, affecting all ranks of society, but having a morbid fascination for more affluent sections of the middle and lower classes. One of the main features would be an impressive cortege, headed by a glass-sided hearse and followed by large numbers of mourning carriages. The horses drawing the hearse would be blacks, usually stallions, imported from Holland and Belgium. These were known as 'Belgian blacks', or by undertakers as 'the black brigade'.

From the 1850s the standard hearse was oblong and obviously coffin-shaped, mounted on elliptical springs fairly high above road level. There would be a box seat for two, with angled footboard and hammercloth, although the latter was frequently an imitation of carved wood. A powerful lever brake acted on the rear wheels. The flat roof would be

Hearse, 1870.

A Canadian hearse, c.1910.

ornamented with black ostrich plumes, one at each corner, but sometimes with a spray in the centre. Each vehicle would have full underlock of the smaller front wheels. Average tare weight would be 17 cwt (864 kg), fairly light for a pair of horses in pole gear, although in poorer districts a single horse in shafts might be used. Hearses used by wealthier families may have had teams of four or more horses, but a well-matched pair was the general rule.

At one period, from the 1880s, there was also an 'elliptical hearse', with near-equirotal wheels, the underside of the bodywork based on a curved or canoe shape similar to the Sefton landau. Side windows were elliptical rather than rectangular. Access to all such vehicles would be through double glass doors at the rear.

Mourners following the hearse rode in what were known as 'mourning carriages', although coach-like and fully enclosed. Rear windows were normally blacked out. A French version of the mourning carriage combined the hearse with a rearward coupé section for mourners. Known as a 'cobillard', it was seldom seen in Britain.

Other vehicles used by undertakers included a small van in which to convey the coffin before a funeral, known as a 'coffin handy', and a four-wheeled 'flower cart' in which wreaths and floral tributes were displayed.

Prison vans

The four-wheeled, fully enclosed prison van, used to take prisoners and their escorts to and from jail or police court, had barred rear windows, a rear entrance door with grab handles and folding steps. This

A rare, 'one-horse' version of the 'black Maria', formerly displayed in Bath.

would be driven to a pair of horses in pole gear, controlled from a seat at or near roof level, with an angled footboard. The small but sturdy forewheels turned in full lock and it was usually mounted on semi-elliptical leaf springs. Many later versions had a clerestory roof for improved lighting and ventilation. Such a vehicle was termed a 'black Maria', so named in honour of Queen Victoria, known to the Cockneys as 'Ria' or 'Maria'. The prototype was introduced during the early years of her reign, painted jet black but with the royal arms and monogram on side panels.

Lifeboat carriages

These were similar to a type of military vehicle used by the Royal Engineers to transport pontoons for temporary bridging purposes. They had large, well-dished artillery wheels and a long wheelbase, but only quarter lock of the forecarriage, with the lifeboat cradled between crosswise bolsters. A team of heavy horses with chain traces would be used to draw the carriage out to sea, where the lifeboat would be floated off in the surge.

Bathing machines

These were tall, box-like vehicles with a door at each end, fairly high above beach level and entered by means of a short ladder. The roofs were either rounded or peaked to a centre ridge for maximum headroom. From a distance they may have resembled a type of gypsy living van or 'vardo', but without windows. Many were decorated with broad vertical stripes in red and white.

The prototype bathing machine was designed for King George III and used by him at Weymouth for sea bathing, a healthy pastime then prescribed as a cure for most ailments. While the bather changed inside the machine, it would be drawn out to sea by a single horse in chain traces, ridden by a man or boy. For the return journey the horse would be taken to the rear of the vehicle and rehitched. Any attempt at turning a bathing machine when surrounded by sea water might have led to an accident.

Vehicles of travelling showmen

Specialised vehicles were widely used by fairground and circus showmen, especially during the second half of the nineteenth century. They were mainly horse-drawn until the 1900s, after which they would be hauled, as part of a road train, by traction engines or motor lorries.

Most beast cages for dangerous performing animals were oblong vehicles, low-slung and equirotal, having suspension of semi-elliptical leaf springs. A driving seat with angled footboard would be at or near roof level. Bars of the cage might be on both sides or one side only, covered by wooden shutters when the animals were no longer on display. Cage wagons would be drawn by a pair of horses in pole gear but sometimes by larger teams, three abreast, unicorn or four-in-hand.

Apart from living quarters for man and beast, there were many wagons needed for props and equipment, most of which were provided by the firm of Savages of King's Lynn, who specialised in showmen's vehicles and fairground attractions. Usually four-wheeled closed vans, those

Showman's living van, 1890s.

Two-roomed saloon-type showman's living van, built by Savage Bros of King's Lynn c.1900.

used for less important parts might be open but high-sided. Wagons containing parts for the steam merry-go-rounds, including the galloping horses or 'gallopers', were known as 'horse trucks'. Even the centre engines that kept the rides spinning, powered steam organs and generated electricity would be mounted on horse-drawn carriages. There were also magnificent tableau wagons, featured in the circus parade, on which human figures, trained animals or gilded statues represented scenes from history, legend and popular literature. The so-called 'Twin Lion Tableau Wagon' of Sir Robert Fossett's Circus had three tiers like a wedding cake and was 17 feet (5 metres) high.

Many showmen had elaborate caravans, some of which were known as 'Burton vans', constructed by a firm at Burton-on-Trent in Staffordshire. These were four-wheeled and fairly high above ground level, nearly equirotal and able to turn in full lock. There would be semi-elliptical leaf springs, front and rear. They were entered through a front door and porch, via steps that could be lowered between the shafts when the horse was detached. It was generally considered that gypsy caravans had larger wheels set further apart than those of showmen, as these were better suited for rutted lanes and rough heathland, while showmen kept to surfaced streets and main roads.

In later years some of the wealthier travelling showmen preferred even larger and more elaborate saloon-type caravans. These would have a longer wheelbase than the Burton vans but were much nearer to ground level, the interiors having partitions for at least two rooms, with free-standing furniture. The doors of such living vans would be at the side rather than front or back, reached by a short flight of steps. Wheels would frequently have a decorative infilling known as a sunburst effect, between the spokes. The saloon van needed at least two horses to move it any distance, although some, like furniture vans, were taken to the station by horses and travelled for most of their journey as part of a goods train.

Gypsy caravans

Although gypsy folk have been wanderers in three continents for over a thousand years, they usually slept in tents or makeshift shelters, their camping equipment carried on the backs of ponies. Early in the nineteenth century, however, some gypsies trading in cheap pottery made use of two-wheeled pot carts not only to display their wares but as bases for demountable tents. The tent became a permanent fixture

Bow-topped caravan

extended to a four-wheeled vehicle, also known as a 'pot cart', drawn by a single horse or large pony. The entrance would be over steps lowered between the shafts. The next stage was to enclose the ends, making the interior more comfortable and secure, and this was first done with canvas. The resulting vehicle was known as the 'open lot'; its undergear was frequently adapted from a trolley or light dray. It was followed by the 'bow-top van', its canvas cover supported on bow-shaped hoops or tilts, blocked off at the ends with solid matchboarding rather than curtains. There would also be a fixed rear window with shutters.

Later, more sophisticated vans, or vardos, had built-in furniture, including cupboards, bed-bunks and patent cooking stoves. These were more spacious than the pot carts and bow-tops and were constructed entirely from matchboards on a framework of upright hardwood standards. They included the 'ledge van', the 'Reading van' and the 'brush van'. The ledge type had sides overhanging the wheels above a waist line. It was also known as the 'cottage van' as it resembled a typical country cottage of the Tudor period, in which a jettied upper storey overhung some distance above the ground floor. The Reading van, even larger and better appointed than the others, was the Rolls-Royce of gypsy caravans, made by a firm of wagon builders based in Reading. It was noted for its elaborate scrollwork and carvings, especially on the supports of the canopy extension of the roof above the front platform. Porches on other types, especially the ledge van, had horizontal supports

Rear view of a ledge van at the Hereford and Worcester County Museum, Hartlebury Castle.

Reading van at the Hereford and Worcester County Museum, Hartlebury Castle.

known as 'feathering'. All types had cupboards, 'belly boxes' or underframe storage space, and sometimes chicken coops built on to the side or rear end. A rearward storage rack, on letting-down chains, was known as a 'cratch'. Suspension would be in the form of semi-elliptical springs. Brush vans, used by makers of brooms, brushes and baskets, mainly in the Fens, were different from other caravans in several important features. The entrance door of this type was at the back rather than the front or side, reached over fixed rather than demountable steps. There were also high rounding boards and room for storage at roof level, while brooms and brushes for sale were kept in side racks. Towards the end of the nineteenth century most vans adopted a clerestory or 'Mollicroft' roof for improved ventilation and lighting.

Gypsy caravans would be drawn by a single horse of the vanner type, although draught might be shared with a 'sider' or second horse attached on the offside by an extension bar. Horses were frequently driven on long reins from the side of the road.

MILITARY VEHICLES

Early military vehicles were based on a dead-axle wagon or cart, often in the care of hired civilian drivers. The most popular type, with a long wheelbase, was the 'Flanders wagon', originating in the Low Countries during the late middle ages. In later years there was a Royal Corps of Wagoners and, in more recent times, the Royal Army Service Corps of soldier-drivers. After disasters in the Crimean War during the 1850s, when more casualties arose from exposure and neglect than from enemy action, there were numerous reforms, especially in the supply and medical services. New transport vehicles were high on the list of priorities, and a special carriage and wagon department was opened at Woolwich Arsenal to design and test a series of two- and four-wheeled types suitable for rigorous conditions in the field.

The most enduring military vehicles of the 1860s were versions of the 'GS' or general service wagon, which was hauled by two or more horses and driven either from a sprung box seat or by mounted drivers on the nearside horses. It was an oblong, plank-sided wagon, usually open but supplied with bale hoops and having a demountable canvas cover. The first mark was introduced in 1862, while marks ten and eleven came in 1905. Average types were about 9 feet (2.7 metres) long, although some used in South Africa and drawn by mules were 13 feet (4 metres) in length. Experiments were made with full underlock and suspension, but the most effective wagons, for both field service and garrison work, were found to be those with limited underlock, dead axles and a strong underperch. Sprung wagons, with smaller forewheels for cut-under, were more awkward and expensive to repair, harder to load (having a higher platform above ground level) and likely to overturn on rutted tracks in the battle area. The GS wagon was mainly used for food supplies and general stores (the bread and meat wagon), although there were eventually large numbers of specialised vehicles (either two- or four-wheeled), including ambulances, water carts, ammunition carts, forge carts, forage carts, wire wagons, pontoon wagons and tool carts or

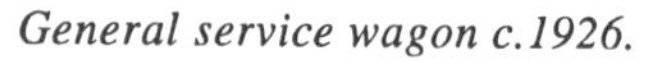

General service wagon c.1926.

wagons (the last mainly used by the Royal Engineers).

During the early twentieth century many transport vehicles supplying mobile cavalry and horse artillery were in the form of limbers or articulated wagons, having almost identical fore and rear bodies, drawn by either two or four horses with mounted drivers. Basically, these were limbered GS wagons mark one of 1906. They were used mainly to save petrol at military bases and camps until the end of the Second World War. They could move faster across country than ordinary wagons, although they could carry only smaller loads and lengthened the line of march.

Carts were less frequently used by the army than wagons. Some carts, however, were essential in rough or mountainous terrain, used in places where wagons might prove awkward and slow. Others were needed for light, short-haul work in and around barracks. These were usually 'Maltese carts', drawn by a small horse, pony or mule, but were sometimes converted into hand carts. They had low sides and slatted floors but could be boarded up for coal, coke or building materials such as sand, lime and cement.

Maltese cart mark 4.

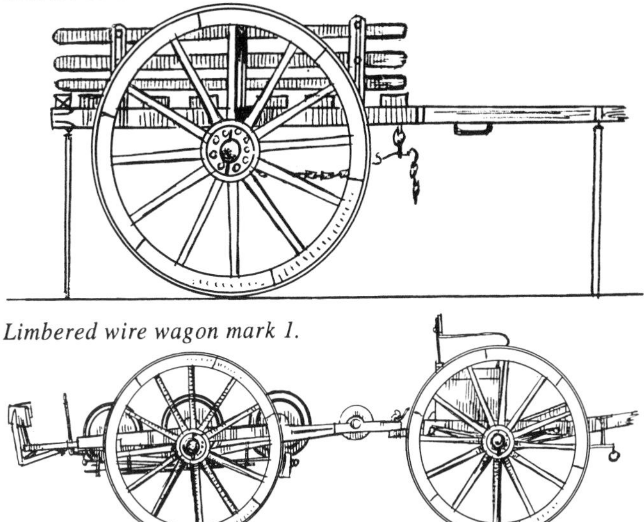

Limbered wire wagon mark 1.

A unique type of military vehicle was the 'limbered wire wagon', dating back to the 1900s. This was used for laying land wires, as opposed to the lumbering, much heavier 'air-line wagon'. First used by the Royal Engineers, but later by their offshoot, the Royal Corps of Signals, it comprised two limbered bodies, both fitted with spools of wire, paid out

Pontoon wagon.

under the control of men seated on either side of the rear limber. It was followed by an outrider with looped staff, whose task was to prevent the wire from snagging. Drawn by teams of four or six horses, this wagon worked at the gallop over rough and undulating ground, laying wire much faster and more efficiently than any of its mechanised successors, either six-wheeled lorries or half-tracks.

Bridging equipment, such as pontoons, would be carried on low-slung wagons, drawn by teams of six horses with mounted drivers. These were similar to the lifeboat carriages mentioned previously. An incongruous detail was a Rogers anchor of the nautical type hanging from the rear of each wagon; this helped to moor pontoons in swiftly flowing rivers.

Travelling cooker.

The mobile or travelling cooker was a limbered vehicle that, until mechanisation, accompanied troops on the line of march; identical types were also used by the Royal Flying Corps. There would be one cooker to 250 men, preparing hot meals while in transit. The forebody or draught limber carried rations and fuel, with pole and swingletrees for connection. It was drawn by a pair of horses controlled by a mounted driver, although versions used by continental armies were usually driven from a box seat, reversing the normal pattern of civilian operations. The rear limber had a stove and four boiler compartments, each lined with asbestos fibre. The tall stove chimney on later types could be lowered to the horizontal when not in use or for passing under low bridges. Food could be kept hot almost indefinitely, served whenever a halt was called or camp pitched. Travelling cookers were last used by the Brigade of Guards in 1940.

One of the more unusual military vehicles in both use and appearance was the mobile pigeon loft. These were introduced in France and Flanders during the First World War, remaining in use until the late 1920s. By 1918 there were over a hundred, used on all parts of the western front. Each four-wheeled van-like vehicle contained about sixty carrier pigeons in the care of a trained NCO and fatigue man. Later pigeon lofts were converted from double-decker omnibuses. The French army had a smaller version mounted on two wheels and drawn by a single horse. Earlier types were either purpose-built or constructed on the underworks of a GS wagon. They were usually drawn by a pair of horses in pole gear, although a few were eventually tractor-hauled. Each vehicle had a single driving seat on the offside of the forecarriage.

Mobile pigeon lofts.

Double entrance doors were at the front of the loft to the right of the driving position, reached by demountable wooden steps. Release cages projected from both sides and rear. Suspension would be semi-elliptical springs, front and rear.

Horse ambulances, for the recovery of sick and wounded horses, were panel-sided carts drawn by a single horse in shafts but sometimes having an extra ridden horse in side gear. With single-horse draught this would be driven from a seat with an angled footboard, fixed above the nearside wheel. A wounded horse entered from the rear over a lowered ramp, which also served as a tailboard. Horses unable to stand were supported by slings hung from steel hoops. Other vertical hoops might be used to frame a canvas top. The horse ambulance was one of the few two-wheeled vehicles to make use of a pedal brake.

Horse ambulance mark II.

FARM VEHICLES

Farm or agricultural vehicles were among the more typical forms of early transport from which many later types developed. It was on early farm wagons in central Europe that a supporting underperch and crude locking devices evolved. However, the lock or turning circle may have been limited by the large front wheels which would have been necessary to support heavy loads over uneven ground. Larger wagons came to depend on sliding metal plates forming, by means of a through pin, a pivot for the forecarriage. Wheel tops entered a waisted recess on opposite sides of the bodywork. Later factory-made vehicles were produced with smaller front wheels, for cut-under in full lock.

The sides of a traditional farm wagon would be based either on a panelled framework or on rows of vertical spindles, with planks fitting horizontally edge to edge. Raves or side boards and end ladders protected an overhanging load. Wheel rims were at first encased in double rows of iron strakes, nailed in position and staggered for greater security. In remote parts of rural England, strakes outlasted iron band tyres, surviving well into the twentieth century. Most wagon wheels were well dished, with conical wooden hubs, fitted to downward inclined axle stubs (axle arms) by flat wedges or linchpins. This method of securing was common to many vehicles and in the novel *Tom Brown's Schooldays* Rugby boys removed the linchpins from the gigs of market folk and farmers as a practical joke.

Most farm wagons had single shafts attached to their forecarriages, although in the eastern counties some had double shafts for two horses working side by side, but not as an attached pair. In east Yorkshire wagons frequently used pole gear for three or more horses, guided by a mounted driver. In most cases, where an extra horse was needed, this would be attached in tandem, heading the shaft horse (wheeler) to save space in narrow places.

In general terms, farm wagons were divided between 'box' and 'bow' types. Box wagons were high-sided but compact, found mainly in the eastern counties, east Midlands and south Yorkshire. Bow wagons had lower sides and longer bodies, with raves arched or bowed above the rear wheels to protect them from overhang. They were found in the Cotswolds, south Midlands and certain parts of the south-west. A variety of box types was distributed throughout the west Midlands, although these had the more pronounced wheel dish and broader treads

East Yorkshire wagon.

Herefordshire wagon.

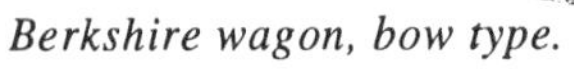

Berkshire wagon, bow type.

Oxfordshire wagon.

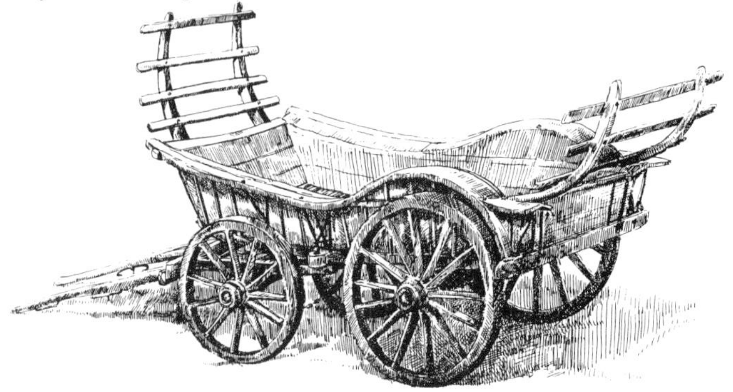

Barge wagon.

associated with bow wagons, especially west of the river Severn. Devon wagons frequently had horizontal rollers above the rear carriage for lashing ropes, which prevented the slipping of high loads in sloping fields. Many county and regional types of wagon developed but very few appeared in Scotland, west Wales, the Pennines or the Lake District. Most early wagons were constructed by local craftsmen or wainwrights. All such vehicles were unsprung or dead-axle, lacking brakes, apart from drag shoe and dogstick.

From the second half of the nineteenth century, factory-made wagons began to appear in large numbers. They were usually 'barge' or 'boat' wagons according to size, having wheels that turned in full lock beneath the undercarriage, thus reducing payload. Full band or ring tyres were then introduced and the hubs and naves were frequently made of cast iron or steel. A flat trolley or dray-like vehicle, often with leaf springs and full lock, was also popular as a factory-produced model of the 1900s.

Carts, although universal for such basic work as manure spreading, were preferred, even for harvesting, in highland districts, while some hill farms used wheel-less drags. In Wales and the Marches there were low-sided wains and 'gambos' on two wheels, some with bowed side protection, while others were mere loading platforms with no upper works of any kind. The so-called tumbrils with large wheels, medium-high sides and rearward tipping gear were drawn by a single horse in shafts, assisted by a chain horse as required. Floorboards set longitudinally rather than crosswise made scraping out easier. This was essential for wet loads such as manure, as cross-boards trapped the moisture that caused warping and decay. Tumbrils, with regional variations, were fairly common in Europe for at least five centuries, also serving as the

Factory-made wagon.

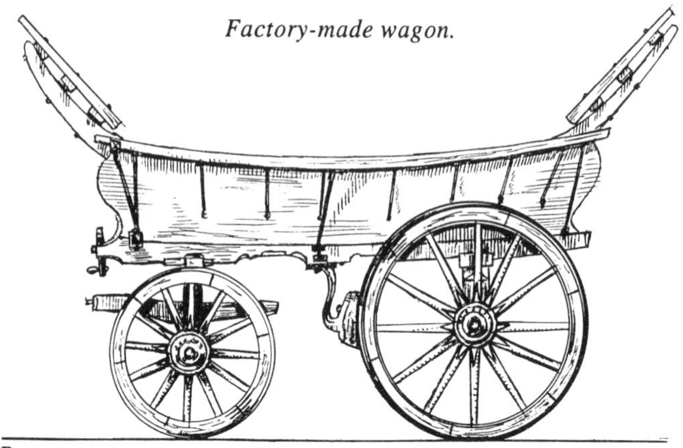

Boat wagon.

prison and execution cart of the French Revolution.

The 'hermaphrodite', once popular on smallholdings, was an economy vehicle, having the rear body of a cart, with a forward extension supported by a detached forecarriage. It could be used as an ordinary cart for most of the year and converted to a harvest wagon in late summer. It was half the price of a wagon.

Logs and lengths of timber were either slung from the underside of a

Early twentieth-century boat wagon.

Carting at the National Shire Horse Centre, Yealmpton, Devon.

two-wheeled framework, known as a 'neb', 'nib', 'bob' or 'pair of wheels', or otherwise conveyed on a four-wheeled carriage or 'timber tug' with end bolsters and stanchions, the ends joined by a centre beam

Northumberland harvest cart.

Hermaphrodite.

Timber bob or neb.

or reach pole. These were drawn by large teams of heavy horses, harnessed in single file, although the wheel horse would be in shafts.

In the Kentish hop fields a special type of wagon was used for harvesting and general purposes; it became known as a 'hop tug'. This had slatted, semi-open sides and high, near-vertical end ladders or corner poles. Most turned in quarter lock only. It was usually drawn by a single horse in shafts, but sometimes assisted by a chain horse.

The 'miller's wagon', not strictly a farm vehicle, was often seen on farms as many millers were also farmers. This type was noted for high loading platforms, medium-high sides and the narrower treads of a road wagon. They would be loaded with bags of grain or flour from an elevated platform or loading bay.

On sheep farms there might have been a four-wheeled shepherd's hut or van that resembled a crudely made caravan. These were driven at lambing time to lonely pastures, where the shepherd would be on duty night and day. Rarely custom-built, unlike more professional vans found in North America and Commonwealth countries, they were roughly assembled from planks of wood and scrap iron, their wheels borrowed from unwanted farm implements. An example formerly at Doddington Carriage Museum (now closed) was converted from an 1890s London horse bus of garden-seat type.

Hop tug or wagon.

Miller's wagon.

8
Vehicles from the United States and other countries

AMERICAN PASSENGER AND PLEASURE CARRIAGES

American vehicles frequently had much in common with British and European types, but there were also unique national developments. Traditional European coaches and carriages appeared mainly in the eastern or Atlantic states, while many new vehicles came with the opening up of the west. These, although not unfamiliar in towns, were originally designed for rural areas and the wide open spaces. Often light but strong, they tended to have large equirotal or near-equirotal wheels. A large number were owner-driven, especially the one-horse, four-wheeled American buggy.

American buggy.

The coalbox buggy

This was a lightweight but strongly built vehicle, its name derived from a grocer's coalbox, seen in village stores and trading posts throughout the nineteenth century. Near-equirotal and mounted on crosswise leaf springs, it was frequently painted red with gold stripes or lining out.

The Jenny Lind

A tray-bodied buggy (like many of its kind) made popular by the

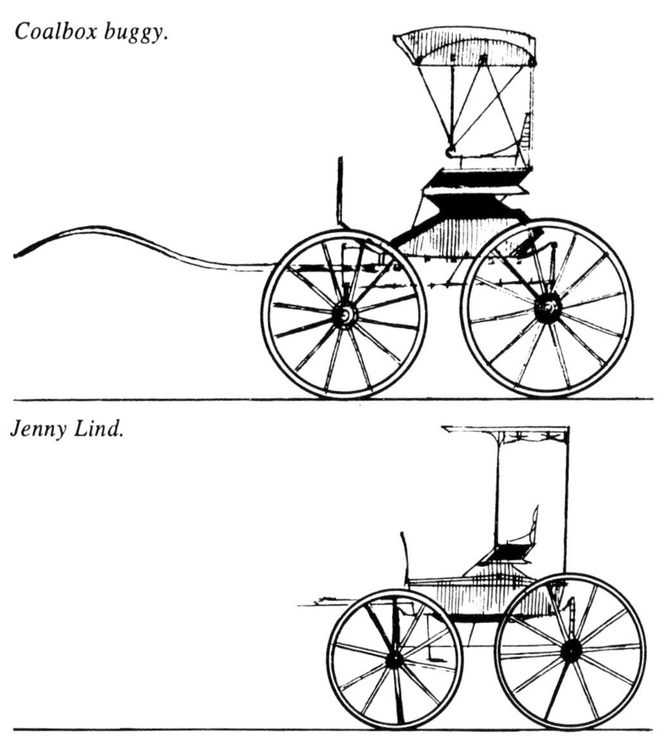

Coalbox buggy.

Jenny Lind.

Swedish opera singer Jenny Lind during her successful tour of the United States, it had a fixed permanent head rather than a falling half-hood.

The business buggy

A smart, elegant vehicle of its type, this had a rear platform for overnight luggage and sample cases. The sides of the shallow body were lined with external canework. It was made with an ample half-hood.

The doctor's wagon or buggy

This vehicle was popular with members of the medical profession, especially in country districts, from the 1890s. The sides of the body-work were caned to waist level. The ample hood had oval side windows. A small rear platform could be used for the medical bag. It was usually painted either black or dark green, with silver mountings, seldom striped or lined out.

The cut-under buggy

This had an arched framework or underbody, to allow full lock. The cross-seat was much higher than with other buggies.

The Amish buggy

The Amish buggy is still used by and made for members of an American religious community who are forbidden to drive mechanically propelled vehicles. It is constructed in the traditional tray-bodied style, with a high front or leather-covered dashboard. It was originally built without a hood, although some modern versions are fully enclosed.

The jump-seat wagon

This light, near-equirotal wagon with a fixed top could be converted from having two rows of seats to a single-seater by 'jumping' or sliding the seats together.

The surrey

The most popular version of the surrey, made famous by the song, was a 'fringe top', its canopy head raised on corner posts or standards and ornamented with deep fringes. A four-wheeled family vehicle, it had open sides with high fenders or mudguards to protect its passengers. It was usually furnished with a double row of well-upholstered seats, fitted rugs and elaborate brass oil lamps. A cheaper version, without a fixed top, was known as the 'spring wagon' or 'poor man's surrey'. The 'pony surrey' was a smaller version, drawn either by a single pony or by a pair in pole gear.

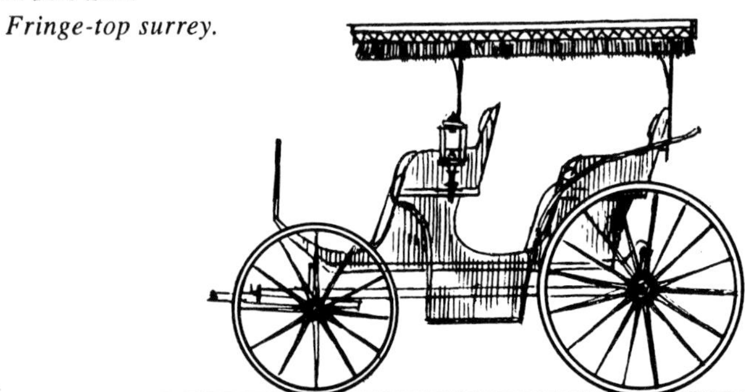

Fringe-top surrey.

The buckboard

A low-slung but strongly made vehicle on four wheels, for overland driving, the buckboard was frequently used on cattle ranches in the far West. It had sturdy but flexible front bracing, which reduced vibration and noise. The only suspension was through flexibility of its shafts and undercarriage. It was drawn by a single horse or large pony.

The rockaway

Also known as the 'depot wagon', this was a four-wheeled vehicle frequently used for taking passengers and their luggage to the nearest railroad depot. It had either two or three rows of crosswise seating, headed and partly enclosed. It measured about 10 feet (3 metres) in length. A ten-seater version, or 'platform wagon', was used at holiday resorts for sightseeing.

The coachee

A type of small stage-coach or public carriage, the coachee was used in and around the larger cities of North America from the late eighteenth to the mid nineteenth century. It was also known as a 'Jersey wagon' as the prototype was first used in the state of New Jersey. Headed but frequently semi-open, with unglazed windows, it was entered from the rear by means of one or two steps. The driver sat under an extension of the roof canopy. Mounted on thoroughbraces rather than metal springs, coachees were limited to half lock only. They were drawn by a pair of medium-light draught horses in pole gear. A larger and much later version, known as the 'coachee-rockaway', seated eight people, at least two more than its predecessor.

Coachee.

The concord

This was a North American version of the long-distance stage-coach, adapted to colonial conditions. It was designed to carry nine inside

Concord, 13 feet (3.9 metres) long.

passengers, with two or three clinging to the roof if allowed by the guard or 'messenger'. It was drawn by a team of six horses, the leading pair harnessed to a separate reach pole. The ovoid or egg-shaped bodywork was suspended on two sets of longitudinal leather straps or thoroughbraces, attached to inflexible metal standards. It was driven from a double roof seat with angled footboard, shared by driver and guard, and named after its place of origin, the New Hampshire town of Concord. Similar vehicles were also exported to Australia and South Africa, where they frequently carried mails.

Connestoga wagon.

FARM, TRADE AND ROAD VEHICLES

Perhaps the most outstanding early vehicles used by settlers in North America, associated with long treks over uninhabited wasteland, were Connestoga wagons. These were the original covered wagons or what later became known as 'prairie schooners', although they were first used as farm and general-purpose wagons in Lancaster County, Pennsylvania. Introduced about 1755, they were first adopted by German settlers or the Pennsylvanian Dutch. The high sides of the Connestoga, with its canvas top spread over hoops, made it an ideal temporary home for purposes of migration. Construction was so sturdy yet flexible that such vehicles could cope with almost any terrain. At first they were dead-axle or unsprung, with panel sides, but later types relied on semi-elliptical leaf springs and hand lever brakes. The large forewheels were restricted to quarter lock only. Some early wagons would be drawn by yoked oxen but most teams comprised four or six horses.

A wide range of both two- and four-wheeled vehicles was used from colonial days until the twentieth century. They frequently had a longer wheelbase than British types while there was less obvious distinction between those needed for farmwork and commercial vehicles on city streets. Carts were seen less frequently than wagons; preferred mainly in the southern states for light plantation work, they were usually dump or tip carts drawn by a small cob-like horse or mule. Those that were used in the northern states were mostly owned by builders and contractors. Straight, low-sided and rarely more than two planks in height, most carts dumped automatically when detached or unhooked at the front. A two-wheeled coal cart, mainly used in small towns on the Atlantic coast, resembled a smaller version of the traditional tumbril.

Four-wheeled wagons used by farmers, contractors and plantation owners were of three or four main types, with near-equirotal wheels, and

American farm wagon c.1900.

American farm wagon.

well-braced with ironwork for rough tracks or badly made roads. A small spring wagon with a shallow or tray-like body and cut-under of the forecarriage would be used for light haulage work, usually drawn by a pair of medium-heavy horses in pole gear. A one-horse wagon of a type still manufactured in fair numbers was long and low-slung but with straight shafts, its driving seat placed above the forecarriage and mounted on crosswise or lengthwise (nutcracker) springs. A low-sided 'mountain wagon', with strong lever brakes, was used in many highland districts, especially on the Pacific seaboard.

In towns and cities numerous drays and open wagons with side stakes or stanchions were used to convey barrels, bales, casks and crates. These were either dead-axle or sprung vehicles, many specially adapted for use by brewers and purveyors of mineral water for street delivery. Town and country timber carriages were similar to those used in Britain, but they often had larger wheels and broader treads; they were known as 'lumber buggies'. Pipes, girders and other loads of excessive length were handled by limbered gear, similar to that found on the timber carriage; vehicles intended for such use had high corner posts at front and rear to keep the load steady.

The ice wagon was a once familiar sight in urban areas. There were two main types: the smaller and perhaps more popular version had cut-under of the forecarriage, high straight sides, a high sprung box seat, a rear door and step with grab handles for access to the interior; it was driven to a pair in pole gear; a larger type, with a capacity of 2 tons, was provided with a rearward canopy or awning, while the semi-enclosed driving seat resembled a half-cab, with side windows. Both types would have the interior fitted out with scales, racks and a range of ice hooks.

The city coal wagon was a large four-wheeled vehicle, with a wooden outer body lined with iron sheeting. There would be a single, elevated

Ice wagon.

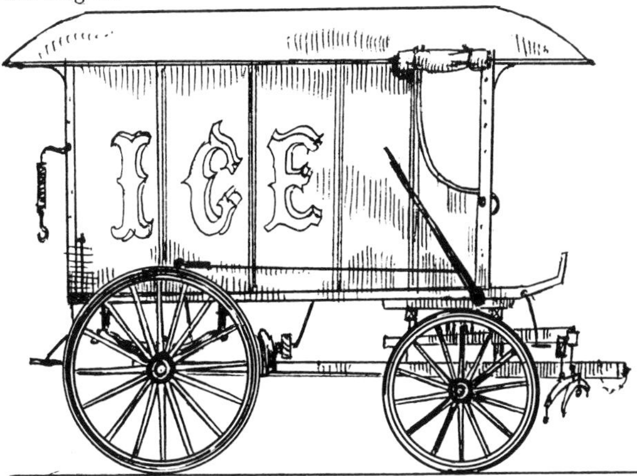

driving seat in a central position above the forecarriage, with an angled footboard. Capacity was 2½ tons. It was drawn by a pair of heavy horses in pole gear. There were both high- and low-sided types, which had full underlock for turning in busy streets and restricted areas.

Trade delivery vans and carts appeared in many different versions from the 1880s. These were usually well-sprung and mounted on either lengthwise or crosswise leaf springs. They would be driven from either an inner semi-enclosed cross-bench or from an open box seat, depending

Milk wagon c.1910.

on style and purpose. One of the most outstanding vehicles was the dairy wagon for distributing bottled milk. This had a step-in mid section, cut-under of the forecarriage, and sliding doors for easy access. The rear body was mounted on transverse springs while the forebody had both crosswise and lengthwise springs united by 'D' links.

The bakery wagon or bread van had a long wheelbase, near-equirotal wheels and half lock of the forecarriage. The rear part was mounted above full elliptical springs on the lengthwise plan, while the forepart relied on a single laminated cross-spring. The enclosed driving position had doors with droplights on each side of the windscreen, with an aperture for the reins. Sliding side panels gave access to the interior.

The butcher's wagon, drawn by a pair of horses, was driven either from the interior or from an outer seat mounted on brackets. It usually had double display windows, with a rearward serving hatch sheltered by a canopy or awning. Floors were of slatted wood, like duckboarding, while interiors were boarded up to the waistline, the upper parts lined with cotton duck, a white, washable material.

North American horse-drawn fire engines were usually constructed on arched irons with full cut-under of the forecarriage. There were four main types, the Gould, the Button, the Silby and the Amoskeag, the last being much larger and longer than the first three and preferred by the New York Fire Department. Apart from the driving seat, vertical pump and boiler, these vehicles were mere carrying frames. Most of the firemen rode on a following tender with spare hose and ladders. Special hose-reel trucks, on two and four wheels, also followed.

Britain and the United States of America were the leading commercial and trading nations during the greater part of the nineteenth century,

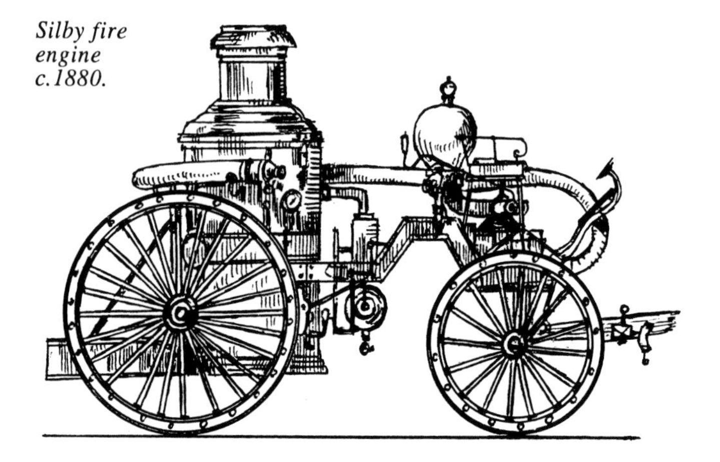

Silby fire engine c.1880.

Continental wagon (Flemish) c.1940.

setting the fashion for most types of horse-drawn vehicle in this area, especially from the 1870s. Among a few notable exceptions were low-slung brewers' drays of German or Scandinavian origins, often with barrels hanging from the underframes. The French also had several unique commercial vehicles, mainly used in Paris. These included a ledge-type wine van for the delivery of small casks, a long-wheelbase open produce van for the sale of fresh vegetables and a pony-drawn butcher's cart, which had a rearward slatted compartment in which a live pig might be carried. These, apart from the butcher's cart, would be drawn by a pair of horses and mounted on semi-elliptical springs. However, cities in five continents had vehicles of both British and North American types.

UNIQUE FOREIGN VEHICLES OF GENERAL TYPE

The Cape cart

A two-wheeled passenger vehicle, hooded and mounted on thoroughbraces, with pole gear for a pair of swift horses, the Cape cart was first used in the Cape Colony of South Africa and later in other dominions and colonies. Its sturdy design and structure made it ideal for military purposes, and large numbers were owned and driven by British officers during the Boer War. There were both front and rear cross-seats with room for three passengers and a driver, as well as ample luggage space.

The carri-coche

The carri-coche was a so-called cart-coach of Brazil used as an omnibus. Drawn by a pair of horses in the care of a postilion, it was mounted on thoroughbraces of untanned oxhide and entered via folding

Cape cart.

steps and a rear door. It seated six passengers, three per side on longitudinal benches, facing inwards.

The coucou

This was a French two-wheeled cab with a pair of crosswise benches. The driver perched on a ledge above an apron-shield of wood or metal. The passengers were referred to as 'rabbits' because they had to crouch

Coucou.

under a fixed hood in the darkened interior. Certain features of the Canadian calèche may have derived from it. The coucou was frequently used in country towns and villages from the late eighteenth century.

The diligence

The name of this vehicle derives from the French word for promptitude, relating to a stage-coach that first ran between Paris and Lyons. It was widely used from the mid eighteenth century to carry both passengers and mail in France and Switzerland, while similar vehicles could be found in Germany and Austria; it was also known as a 'post coach'. The driver occupied a seat at or near roof level, shared with several passengers. There was also a cross-seat further back, protected by a half-hood, known as a 'banquette'. Teams of up to five horses were frequently used, one of the leaders often ridden by a postilion.

The ekka

A two-wheeled passenger or pleasure cart of India, the ekka was drawn by a single pony. The original version, later improved for the use of British military officers and civil servants, was large enough for a driver and single passenger only. Draught gear was in the form of a pole above the hind quarters of the pony, secured by means of breast straps. A larger version, drawn by a pair of ponies, was known as the 'tonga', having back-to-back seating.

The kibitka

A primitive Russian version of the post coach, used for over two centuries, this was a four-wheeled vehicle but lacked any form of suspension. In later versions passengers sat on cushions stuffed with hay above rope hammocks. The top or head was of heavy-duty canvas stretched over hoops. An even larger but slower version was known as the 'oboze'.

The stolkjaerre

This two-wheeled cab from Norway was used as a travelling carriage, and drawn by a large pony or single horse of the 'fiord' type driven from a low-slung rearward seat below passenger level. Two passengers faced forward at the front of the vehicle, in the style of a hansom cab.

The volante

A two-wheeled vehicle originating in Spain, the volante was used from the mid eighteenth century mainly in Latin America and the West Indies, especially Cuba. The seats were well in advance of the large carrying wheels, below axle level. There was room for two or three passengers facing forward. Usually hooded and mounted on 'C' springs, it was drawn by three horses abreast, one ridden by a postilion.

The wurst wagon

A German hunting wagon, unsprung or dead-axle and mounted on four wheels, this vehicle was long and narrow like a *Wurst* or German sausage. It was ridden astride by members of a hunting or shooting party, their feet sharing a common footboard on either side.

MODERN SPORTING AND EXERCISE VEHICLES

Since the early 1970s there has been an increased interest in competitive driving at all levels including three-day events with cross-country hazards, and scurry driving, that is, in a show ring between obstacles. This has led to the introduction of a whole range of vehicles adapted for these purposes. They include both two- and four-wheeled types, although only four-wheeled 'phaeton' style vehicles are eligible for international three-day events. Outstanding features are the use of all-steel wheels with welded spokes, coil-spring shock absorbers, a framework of tubular steel and many details, including hubs, of cast epoxy resin. Hubs are frequently flat or of low profile to avoid scraping objects that might both damage the vehicle and earn penalty points in certain contests. A trend-setter in this area was the 'Daresbury phaeton' of the early 1980s, which had hydraulic disc brakes, coil suspension and a unique spare wheel, its framework being of hollow metal construction throughout.

There are also low-slung exercise carts for either horses or ponies, of tubular steel section, many with wire-spoked and rubber-tyred wheels more like bicycle wheels. Versions of these, mounted on cranked axles, have also been adapted for the use of disabled drivers, with rearward ramps that can be lowered to allow access for wheelchairs.

A typical lightweight exercise cart for training purposes, now appearing in a wide range of sizes, may be dismantled for transportation over long distances. Wheels, shafts and suspension are all removable, although a novice might assemble them in less than ten minutes. Wheels may be moved to any position along the frame, to achieve the desired focus of balance.

9
Builders, materials and finish

The trade of building coaches and carriages eventually employed many craftsmen and highly skilled workers, ranging from heraldic painters to body makers or builders, wheelwrights and lamp makers. Although most of the parts were originally made under the same roof, there was a growing tendency, from the middle of the eighteenth century, towards specialisation. This led to sub-contracts for many fittings, including axles, springs and brakes.

Some builders specialised in certain types of vehicle and were unable or unwilling to produce anything very different from that to which they were accustomed. Sharp & Bland of South Audley Street, London, specialised in larger, heavier vehicles and were unable to satisfy Lord Brougham when he commissioned them to construct a small neat closed carriage for personal town use. The order was later transferred to Robinson & Cook of Mount Street, with satisfactory results.

Farm wagons and carts were usually constructed by local craftsmen known as wainwrights. Although essentially joiners, they were skilled in the fashioning of both wood and metal, working in close co-operation with blacksmiths and specialist wheelwrights. From the mid nineteenth century factory production gradually predominated and standards of local craftsmanship tended to decline. Crude mass-production methods were soon applied to most types of horse-drawn vehicle, including the numerous vans and carts of trade or commerce. While some of the superior coach and carriage builders, mainly based in London and a few larger cities, continued to cater for the wealthier classes, smaller, often owner-driven vehicles were manufactured in much the same way as the family cars that succeeded them. Press advertisements, deferred payment, cash on delivery and production-line assembly applied as much to gig and tub cart as to Model T Fords. Many large organisations, including railway companies and co-operative societies, ran their own vehicle repair and assembly shops, turning out a variety of carts, wagons and vans according to need. During the world wars these centres also produced many vehicles, such as supply wagons, for military purposes.

Basic materials

Just as a variety of skills was represented in vehicle construction, so a number of different materials were also used. The chief of these were wood and metal, used for bodies, wheels and undercarriages.

Ash and oak were the most valued timbers, especially when grown in hedge or coppice. Ash was used mainly for the framework of the body, being tough, fibrous and lacking elasticity, making it unlikely to warp. Oak, usually of young growth, was used for underframes and wheel spokes. Elm was ideal for planks, wheel hubs or naves but, having a strongly marked grain, was difficult to paint. Mahogany could be used for both interior or exterior panels and was favoured for its attractive grain and smooth surface. If panels were to be covered by leather or fabric, however, a cheaper cedar wood might be introduced as a replacement.

At first the metal parts were chiefly made of iron; it was used for bars, hoops, stays, axles, tyres and plates. Eventually steel began to replace iron in many of its functions, especially for tyres. Iron tyres tended to crack and flake much sooner than those of steel. Copper was used for beading and sheathing, while buckles, rings, plates and door handles were made of brass. Superior axle nuts would be made of gun-metal. Other metals and alloys were used for decorative work and small accessories.

Farm vehicles and heavier commercial types depended mainly on an oak framework and undergear, reinforced with minimum strapping. As an alternative, axletrees of large wagons were frequently made of beechwood. Side panels would be of oak or poplar, and planks of elm. Pinewood was frequently used for the side panels of delivery vans, although the better-class vehicles had mahogany panels, produced to much the same standards as carriages.

Upholstery and paintwork

The interior trim of coaches and passenger vehicles related to well-fitting seats of maximum comfort, upholstered according to individual taste or the fashions of the day. Leather was one of the more traditional forms of upholstery, but by the middle of the eighteenth century there was a preference for figured tabaret (a silk stuff with alternating stripes of satin and watered surface, much favoured by coach makers and furnishers) and a variety of hard-wearing satins. From the late 1870s there was a revival of leather coverings and the finest-quality upholstery was produced in Morocco leather. Side curtains were made of silk lutestring, a stiff, satin-surfaced material. The floors of enclosed vehicles were covered with Brussels carpeting or fitted velvet pile rugs. The living vans of travelling folk had floor coverings of oilcloth and linoleum, with quality carpets for those able to afford them.

Exterior paintwork was an important aspect of vehicle construction, especially for the coaches and carriages of wealthier customers. It affected not only the appearance of the vehicle, but also its durability. First many coats of paint, alternately white lead and yellow ochre, were laid on as quickly as possible. When these had hardened thoroughly, after two or three weeks, all the paintwork was rubbed down with pumice stone and water until the grain and brush marks were eliminated and the surface was entirely smooth. Two further coats of white lead paint were then applied and rubbed down with sandpaper. The main body colours of green, brown and so on were then painted over the sanded surfaces; up to three coats could be applied. Afterwards the metal frames and underparts were blackened and allowed to dry, before the application of at least six coats of copal varnish. Two qualities of varnish were used, the better and harder reserved for wheels and undercarriage. As a final touch, before varnishing, all unplated metal parts were japanned. At least eighteen to twenty coats of paint were used for a first-class job. After the vehicle had been used for several months, perhaps half a year, the brilliant gloss, especially on body panels or quarters, would be revived by further hand polishing. This would be done by a professional polisher using a mixture of oil and rottenstone, a decomposed form of siliceous limestone, deprived of its calcareous or chalky matter, and widely used as a polishing agent for both metal and paintwork.

Lamps

Lamps were square or round. Most were originally lit by candles of beeswax, but later oil and even battery lamps were used. The best-quality wax candles were preferred for private vehicles, although delivery vans and carts used cheaper tallow candles. Both types fitted into tinplate tubes, forced gradually upwards by coiled springs as they burned down. Candle lamps were always reliable and much cleaner than oil lamps.

Cart lamps, sometimes used on heavier commercial vehicles, were mainly square with rounded tops, having protective bars across the lens.

10
Glossary

Axle, axle arm: spindle upon which a wheel turns.

Axle box: box-like structure; part of a wheel into which an axle might be fitted.

Axletree: there are two main types, one in which the axle is supported by a wooden beam or tree, and another in which wheels are attached to arms or 'stubs' at each end of the tree.

Bale hoops: hoops or tilts on a vehicle supporting a waterproof cover.

Boot: locker under, or forming part of, the driving seat on a horse-drawn vehicle; any type of luggage compartment.

Box: raised driving seat above the forecarriage of a vehicle. It could be double or single and formerly contained either a tool kit or valuables.

Carriage: a medium to light passenger vehicle, usually open or semi-open, running on four wheels (exceptions are the curricle and the cabriolet). The underparts or running gear of a vehicle. In general terms, any type of vehicle suitable for transport.

Carriage parts: components of undergear or undercarriage on any vehicle.

Chamfer: the trimming or spoke-shaving of wheels and bodywork on a vehicle to reduce its overall weight and for decorative purposes.

Collets: metal bands securing the hubs on certain vehicles, especially those with 'collinge' hubs or axles.

Cranes: iron underframes of a coach or carriage; they were curved or raised to allow better underlock of the forewheels.

Cranked axle: axle cranked or bent to carry a heavy load with low clearance. This made the interior or platform lower for greater ease of loading.

Curricle gear: centre pole in certain forms of double harness, attached to the saddle pads of a pair by means of T-shaped bars and rollers.

Dashboard: raised vertical shield, often leather-covered, at the front of a vehicle, protecting the driver from mud or grit thrown up by the hoofs of the horses in draught.

Dish: the inward or concave slope of wheel spokes, giving the wheel a cone-shaped appearance.

Drag shoe: hollow metal plate used as a scotch under the nearside rear wheel of a four-wheeled vehicle on downward gradients.

Equirotal: describes the wheels of a vehicle that are of equal size, front and back.

Fellowes: outer sections of a wheel, supporting the tyre, and to which spokes are also fitted; pronounced 'fellies'.

Footboard: angled board to support the feet of a driver; also used by passengers on a jaunting car and dogcart.

Futchell, futchel: prong-like fittings on the forecarriage of a horse-drawn vehicle, to which shafts are attached.

Hammercloth: protective and decorative cover on the box seat of certain coaches and carriages; noted for its deep fringes and elaborate embroidery.

Hammercloth coach: a formal or dress coach making use of a hammercloth; usually a privately owned vehicle of superior quality.

Headed: (of a vehicle) enclosed with a head or roof.

Hermaphrodite: compromise vehicle between a cart and wagon, having a detachable forecarriage. It cost half as much as an ordinary wagon.

Hub: centre part of a wheel, into which an axle or axle arm or stub fits; of either wood or metal.

Ladder: rack-like end support, on cart or wagon. Used mainly at harvest time to protect an overhanging load.

Leaf springs: springs made from laminated iron or steel plates. They appear in either elliptical or semi-elliptical form.

Linchpin: a flat wedge shape, securing certain types of wheel to their axles.

Lock: the angle through which the forewheels of a vehicle turn.

Mail hub or axle: patent hub first used on mail coaches, holding the wheel in place with three long screws that were unlikely to snap at the same time.

Nave: the centre of a wheel hub, also an alternative name for the hub.

Park coach or drag: private coach, similar to a stage or mail coach, driven by an amateur whip.

Perch, underperch: beam or bar supporting the underbody of a vehicle in longitudinal form; a connection between front and rear carriages; seldom used on medium and smaller vehicles after the introduction of leaf springs.

Pipe box: metal-lined wheel centre for nave or hub.

Pole: draught pole or beam to which a pair of horses may be harnessed, one on each side, to draw a coach, carriage or wagon. The head of a coach pole terminated in a large elongated hook, while the carriage pole had two small loops and the wagon pole had a large single loop.

Propstick: carried at either end of a vehicle, especially two-wheeled types, to support its weight in a resting position, with horses shut out.

Rave: side board or extension of a cart or wagon to protect the wheel tops from an overhanging load.

Roller bolt: small upright bollard to which the traces of coach harness may be attached for draught purposes; fitted in pairs to a splinterbar on either side of a draught pole.

Rumble: rearward seat on a coach or carriage, usually for grooms or footmen acting as carriage servants; also found on early stage-coaches as a rearward basketwork compartment for passengers travelling at cheaper rates.

Shafts: pair of curved or straight bars to which a single horse might be attached for draught purposes; usually single but some farm wagons of the eastern counties had double shafts.

Skid pan: alternative name for a drag shoe; known in country districts as a 'drugbat'.

Splinterbar: horizontal, transverse beam at the front of a vehicle, to which shafts, roller bolts or swingletrees were attached for draught purposes.

Swingletree: see *Whippletree.*

Thills: traditional country name for shafts.

Tooling: driving a pair or team of horses.

Tyre, tire: metal band fixed to the outer rim of a wheel. Later tyres, especially on passenger vehicles, were made of solid rubber. Pneumatic tyres had a limited period of use for farm and trade vehicles from the 1930s.

Underperch: see *Perch.*

Wain: traditional or country name for a wagon; also a primitive, low-slung harvest cart, usually having bowed protection over the wheels.

Wainwright: a builder or repairer of wagons, especially in country districts.

Whippletree: horizontal draught bar to which the traces of a draught horse might be attached; usually hooked to a loop on the splinterbar; also known as a swingletree.

Yandell top: patent folding hood, with a downward curve at the fore-end, used on American buggies.

British terms and American equivalents

British	*American*
Axle box	Bush
Bond	Hub-band
Dashboard or dash	Splashboard
Dogstick	Dragstaff or mountain point
Float	Light wagon or floater
Gammon seat or Gammon board	Top seat
Head	Fixed top
Headboard	Top bar
Hood or canopy	Bonnet
Limber	Caisson
Lining	Striping
Locking plate	Bedplate
Mudguard or splasher	Fender
Patent leather	Glazed leather
Pillow	Front bolster
Pole (draught pole)	Tongue
Tailboard	Tailgate
Telegraph springs	Mail springs
Timber carriage or tug	Lumber buggy
Wingnut	Thumbnut

In Britain the term 'buggy' is applied to a two-wheeled gig, but in the United States a buggy is a four-wheeled vehicle.

11
Further reading

Army Service Corps Training. Part Three (Transport). HMSO, 1911.
Arnold, James. *Farm Wagons of England and Wales*. John Baker, 1969.
Arnold, James. *All Drawn by Horses*. David & Charles, 1979.
Bird, Anthony. *Roads and Vehicles*. Longmans, 1969.
Burgess, J.W. *A Practical Guide to Coach Building*. London, 1918.
Croal, Thomas A. *A Book About Travelling, Past and Present*. William P. Nimmo, London and Edinburgh, 1877.
Damase, Jacques. *Carriages*. Weidenfeld & Nicolson, 1968.
Edwards, Lionel. *Thy Servant the Horse*. Country Life, 1952.
Evans, Geraint. *The English Farm Wagon*. Oakwood Press for the University of Reading, 1969.
Lang, Jennifer. *An Assemblage of 19th Century Horses and Carriages*. With coloured illustrations by William F. Freelove. Perpetua Press, 1971.
Parry, David. *English Horse-drawn Vehicles*. Frederick Warne, 1952.
Rittenhouse, Jack D. *American Horse-drawn Vehicles*. Crown Publishers, New York, 1958.
The Royal Mews, Buckingham Palace. The Official Guide. Pitkin Pictorials, 1964.
Smith, D.J. *Discovering Horse-drawn Transport of the British Army*. Shire, 1977.
Smith, D.J. *Discovering Horse-drawn Caravans*. Shire, 1981.
Smith, D.J. *Collecting and Restoring Horse-drawn Vehicles*. Patrick Stephens, 1984.
Smith, D.J. *Discovering Horse-drawn Carriages*. Shire, third edition 1985.
Smith, D.J. *Discovering Horse-drawn Commercial Vehicles*. Shire, second edition 1985.
Smith, D.J. *A Dictionary of Horse-drawn Vehicles*. J. A. Allen, 1988.
Sturt, George (George Bourne). *The Wheelwright's Shop*. Cambridge University Press, 1963.
Sumner, Philip. *Carriages to the End of the 19th Century*. Science Museum Booklet, HMSO, 1970.
Tarr, Lazlo. *The History of Carriages*. Vision Press and Corvina Press, London and Budapest, 1969.
Thompson, John (compiler). *Horse-drawn Heavy Goods Vehicles*. John Thompson, Fleet, 1977.
Vince, John. *Discovering Carts and Wagons*. Shire, third edition 1987.
Ward-Jackson, C.H., and Harvey, Dennis. *The English Gypsy Caravan*. David & Charles, 1972.
Watney, Marylian. *The Elegant Carriage*. J. A. Allen, 1961, reprinted 1971.

Watney, Marylian and Sanders. *Horse Power.* Hamlyn, 1975.

Magazines and journals

Carriage Journal (quarterly): obtainable only by subscription from the Carriage Association of America, 885 Forest Avenue, Portland, Maine, USA.

Carriage Driving (bi-monthly): Richard James, Willingdon Management Ltd, 22 Bedwin Street, Salisbury, Wiltshire SP1 3UT.

The Field (weekly): 8 Stratton Street, London W1X 6AT.

Heavy Horse World (quarterly): Park Cottage, West Dean, Chichester, West Sussex PO18 0RX.

Horse and Hound (weekly): High Holborn, London W1X 6AT.

Riding: The Horse Lover's Magazine (monthly): 189 High Holborn, London WC1V 7BA.

12
Places to visit

Before making a special journey, intending visitors are advised to check the times of opening and also that horse-drawn vehicles will be on display.

Avon

Bristol Industrial Museum, Princes Wharf, Prince Street, Bristol BS1 4RN. Telephone: 0272 251470.

Bedfordshire

The Shuttleworth Collection, Old Warden Aerodrome, Biggleswade SG18 9ER. Telephone: 0767 627288.

Stockwood Craft Museum and Gardens, Stockwood Country Park, Farley Hill, Luton LU1 4BH. Telephone: 0582 38714. Incorporates the Mossman Collection of Horse-drawn Wheeled Vehicles.

Berkshire

Courage Shire Horse Centre, Cherry Garden Lane, Maidenhead Thicket, Maidenhead SL6 3QD. Telephone: 0628 824848.

The Rural History Centre (incorporating Museum of English Rural Life), The University, Whiteknights, Reading RG6 2AG. Telephone: 0734 318660.

Cheshire

Gawsworth Hall, Gawsworth, Macclesfield SK11 9RN. Telephone: 0260 223456.

Cornwall

Cornish Shire Horse Trust and Carriage Museum, Lower Gryllis, Treskillard, Redruth TR16 6LA. Telephone: 0209 713606.

Derbyshire

Red House Stables, Old Road, Darley Dale DE4 2ER. Telephone: 0629 733583.

Devon

Arlington Court, Arlington, near Barnstaple EX31 4LP. Telephone: 0271 850296.

Buckland Abbey, Yelverton PL20 6EY. Telephone: 0822 853607.

Dorset

Dorset Heavy Horse Centre, Grains Hill, Edmondsham, Verwood BH21 5RJ. Telephone: 0202 824040.

Durham

Beamish: The North of England Open Air Museum, Beamish DH9 0RG. Telephone: 0207 231811.

Raby Castle, Staindrop, Darlington DL2 3AH. Telephone: 0833 60202.

Gloucestershire

Cotswold Countryside Collection, Fosseway, Northleach GL54 3JH. Telephone: 0451 860715.

Gloucester Transport Museum, Bearland, Gloucester GL1 2JW. Telephone: 0452 526467. The vehicles may be viewed from outside the building.

Hampshire

Breamore Countryside Museum, Breamore, Fordingbridge SP6 2DF. Telephone: 0725 22468.

Hereford and Worcester

Hereford and Worcester County Museum, Hartlebury Castle, Hartlebury, near Kidderminster DY11 7XZ. Telephone: 0299 250416.

Humberside

Museum of Army Transport, Flemingate, Beverley HU17 0NG. Telephone: 0482 860445.

Normanby Park Farming Museum, Normanby Hall Country Park, Normanby, Scunthorpe DN15 9HU. Telephone: 0724 720588.

Streetlife – Hull Museum of Transport, High Street, Hull. Telephone: 0482 593902. Only two vehicles currently on show; a major new exhibition will open in 1995.

Isle of Wight

Brickfields Horsecountry, Newnham Road, Binstead, near Ryde PO33 3TH. Telephone: 0983 66801.

Kent

Tyrwhitt-Drake Museum of Carriages, Archbishop's Stables, Mill Street, Maidstone ME15 6YE. Telephone: 0622 754497.

Leicestershire

Snibston Discovery Park, Ashby Road, Coalville LE6 2LN. Telephone: 0530 510851.

London

Gunnersbury Park Museum, Gunnersbury Park, London W3 8LQ. Telephone: 081-992 1612.

Hampton Court Palace, East Molesey, Surrey KT8 9AU. Telephone: 081-977 8441.

London Transport Museum, 39 Wellington Street, Covent Garden, London WC2E 7BB. Telephone: 071-379 6344.

Museum of London, London Wall, London EC2Y 5HN. Telephone: 071-600 3699. The Lord Mayor's coach.

The Royal Mews, Buckingham Palace Road, London SW1W 0QH. Telephone: 071-799 2331.

Science Museum, Exhibition Road, South Kensington, London SW7 2DD. Telephone: 071-938 8000.

Merseyside

Liverpool Museum, William Brown Street, Liverpool L3 8EN. Telephone: 051-207 0001.

Norfolk

Cockley Cley Iceni Village and Museums, Cockley Cley, Swaffham PE37 8AG. Telephone: 0760 721339 or 24588.

North Yorkshire

Castle Howard, York YO6 7DA. Telephone: 065384 333.

York Castle Museum, Tower Street, York YO1 1RY. Telephone: 0904 653611.

Yorkshire Museum of Carriages and Horse-drawn Vehicles, Yore Mill, by Aysgarth Falls, Aysgarth DL8 3SR. Telephone: 0748 823275.

Nottinghamshire

Nottingham Industrial Museum, Courtyard Buildings, Wollaton Park, Nottingham NG8 2AE. Telephone: 0602 284602.

Staffordshire

Bass Museum, Visitor Centre and Shire Horse Stables, Horninglow Street, Burton upon Trent DE14 1JZ. Telephone: 0283 511000 or 42031.

Shugborough, Milford, Stafford ST17 0XB. Telephone: 0889 881388 extension 211.

Suffolk

Museum of East Anglian Life. Abbotts Hall, Stowmarket IP14 1DL. Telephone: 0449 612229.

Warwickshire

Charlecote Park, Wellesbourne, Warwick CV35 9ER. Telephone: 0789 470277.

Ragley Hall, Alcester B49 5NJ. Telephone: 0789 762090.
The Shakespeare Countryside Museum at Mary Arden's House, Station Road, Wilmcote, Stratford-upon-Avon CV37 9UN. Telephone: 0789 204016.

West Midlands
The Black Country Museum, Tipton Road, Dudley DY1 4SQ. Telephone: 021-557 9643.

West Yorkshire
Shibden Hall and Folk Museum of West Yorkshire, Listers Road, Halifax HX3 6XG. Telephone: 0422 352246.

Isle of Man
Manx Museum, Douglas. Telephone: 0624 675522.

Scotland
Glasgow Museum of Transport, Kelvin Hall, 1 Bunhouse Road, Glasgow G3 8PZ. Telephone: 041-357 3929.
Hamilton District Museum, 129 Muir Street, Hamilton, Lanarkshire ML3 6BJ. Telephone: 0698 283981.

Wales
Welsh Folk Museum, St Fagans, Cardiff CF5 6XB. Telephone: 0222 569441.

Northern Ireland
Ulster-American Folk Park, Mellon Road, Castletown, Omagh, County Tyrone BT78 5QY. Telephone: 0662 243292 or 243293.
Ulster Folk and Transport Museum, Cultra, Holywood, County Down BT18 0EU. Telephone: 0232 428428.

Republic of Ireland
The Guinness Museum, St James's Gate Brewery, Dublin 8. Telephone: (01) 756701 extension 190.

Index

Page numbers in italic refer to illustrations